CW00472935

A HANDBOOK FOR
CATECHISTS

Hannah Vaughan-Spruce

*All books are published
thanks to the generosity of the supporters
of the Catholic Truth Society*

About the Author

Hannah Vaughan-Spruce is the national coordinator of Divine Renovation UK, a ministry that helps parish priests and lay leaders round the world move their parishes from maintenance to mission. She is currently undertaking PhD research at the Benedict XVI Centre for Religion and Society on parish culture and evangelisation. She is an experienced catechist, author of the Confirmation programme, *Transformed in Christ*, and has worked in evangelisation and catechesis at both parish and diocesan level for ten years.

Acknowledgements

I have a debt of gratitude to several people for their teaching and conversations, and for equipping me as a catechist and evangelist. The Maryvale Institute was an incredible place to study part-time as I worked in a parish. It was here that my knowledge and understanding of the mission of catechesis in the Church was nourished and grew, and I owe huge thanks especially to Dr Petroc Willey and Dr Caroline Farey. So much of my understanding of catechetics is thanks to their teaching and my conversations with them. Finally, the last few years have seen great waves in the Church caused by Sherry Weddell's 2012 book, *Forming Intentional Disciples*. My understanding of the thresholds of conversion is thanks to what I have learnt, not only from this book, but also from conversations on the Forming Intentional Disciples Forum, and from conversations with Sherry Weddell and Katherine Coolidge of the Catherine of Siena Institute. It is a privilege to learn from such experts in the vineyard.

Published 2018 by The Incorporated Catholic Truth Society
40-46 Harleyford Road London SE11 5AY
Tel: 020 7640 0042 Fax: 020 7640 0040
© The Incorporated Catholic Truth Society.

ISBN 978 1 78469 554 5

Contents

How To Use this Handbook

In 2016 a friend of mine – let's call her Sophie – left the big smoke of London with her young family and moved into a new house in the suburbs. She started attending her local Catholic church and enjoyed its family-friendly environment. Before long, Sophie filled out a new parishioners' card, dutifully ticking one or two of the skills boxes, hoping to help in some way. She also wrote that she had attended an adult formation programme in her previous parish. Sophie had not been home for ten minutes after handing in the card when the phone rang. Someone from the parish was at the end of the line, explaining that the parish needed a Baptism catechist. Would she help? After all, she had mentioned adult formation on her card. Sophie agreed to consider it. She had had no training or experience as a catechist. And yet, a week later, where did she find herself, but sitting in one of the parish rooms with a group of parents, shakily explaining the Sacrament of Baptism.

How did you end up being a catechist? Perhaps you are seasoned in this work and experience your role as a vocation. Or maybe you have reluctantly stepped up and feel unsure about what is required. However you ended up here, this handbook is designed to support you.

In September 2013, I was in Rome for the Day for Catechists. On the last day, we were uplifted as Pope Francis entered the auditorium and spoke about the vocation of being a catechist:

> Even if at times it may be difficult and require a great deal of work, and although the results are not always what we hope for, teaching the faith is something beautiful! It is perhaps the best legacy we can pass on: the faith!...Catechesis is a

vocation: "being a catechist"...is something that embraces our whole life. It means leading people to encounter Christ by our words and our lives, by giving witness.

(Address to Catechists, Friday 27 September, 2013)

In Pope Francis's words, catechesis is not just a job we do on a Sunday, but "something that embraces our whole life". At the heart of being a catechist is your relationship with God. As you learn more about what God is calling you to, we hope this handbook will accompany you on a journey of personal spiritual renewal. Make your own notes, use the journal prompts, dive into Scripture, and bring the questions to prayer. The more we put into our own growth as disciples, the more we will have to pass on to others.

Key Guide

PONDER	JOURNAL PROMPT	RECAP	READ	CATECHIST TESTIMONY
A question to reflect on	Write about your own thoughts and reactions	Check you have understood key points	Further reading to find out more	Catechists share their own experience

PART 1
Catechesis: The Essentials

CHAPTER 1

The Church Exists To Evangelise

IN THIS CHAPTER...

• Consider what challenges secularisation has posed to the Church and how the context in which we give catechesis is changing.

• Consider what is the main message God wants us to share.

That moment of honesty

I remember it clearly. The group of fourteen-year-old girls sat around a long table in one of our parish rooms. It was the final session before their Confirmation Mass and the discussion had turned to what they were planning to wear. I tried to steer it back towards the topic at hand – how they were going to continue growing in faith once they had been confirmed. Then one girl piped up with perhaps the most honest thing she had said all year: "I'm not sure I even believe in God, you know." It hit me like plunging into ice-cold water – it took my breath away. In one and the same moment I loved that this girl had finally and honestly said what was on her mind, but I was hit by the realisation that we had ploughed so much effort and time into a course – week after week – only to produce...this: a teenage girl who wasn't sure she believed God existed but nevertheless had a beautiful outfit ready for the Confirmation Mass the following week. She was having no second thoughts about going through with it.

Have you ever had a moment like this in your catechesis, when a situation or conversation woke you up to a reality that was hard to ignore – that what you had been doing had not been achieving the results you had hoped?

- *What has been your experience of giving catechesis?*
- *What fruitfulness have you seen that you give God thanks for?*
- *What failures have you experienced that have discouraged you?*

Waking the sleeping giant: secularisation and the Church

On a far wider scale, the Church in the West is going through its own waking-up process. Statistics tell us the impact of secularisation on Christianity has been like acid, corroding what we thought would stand forever. 48.5 per cent of the British population describe themselves as having "no religion" – they are what sociologists call religious "nones".[1] This makes our society one of the most secular in the West, and it goes without saying that the culture we live in is a harsh environment for Christian faith to survive in.

What about inside the Catholic Church itself? Our conversion rate is low compared to other Christian traditions – only 7.7 per cent of current Catholics were not brought up Catholic. Our lapsation rate is high: for every one Catholic convert there are ten cradle Catholics who no longer regard themselves to be Catholic. 59.6 per cent of all cradle Catholics say they never or practically never attend church.[2]

We are facing challenges both inside and outside: outside, the environment in which the Church exists is hostile to and erosive of Christian faith; inside, the Church is failing to transmit faith that can withstand the acid of secularisation. Some sociologists predict that the likelihood of Christianity reversing the trend, turning the ship around in this late stage of secularisation, is very slim.[3]

Imagine that a new trend were to spring up among your circle of friends – maybe a new fitness programme, diet craze or lifestyle accessory. Studies show that people adopt a new idea only when those who are already following it are similar to them, only more successful and happy.[4]

Imagine, then, if we were to apply this to religion. Like any other cultural phenomenon, for someone to become a Christian it is likely they know others who explicitly live their Christian faith, and they consider those people happier and more successful than themselves.

What would it take to reverse the spiral of Christian decline? Perhaps hordes of passionate Christians contagiously sharing their faith with their peers. A cultural movement on a vast scale.

Sociologists predict that such a phenomenon would be highly improbable. Most evidence suggests that the chips are stacked against us. But we believe in a God who consistently chose the weak to demonstrate his power to the strong and who sent out fishermen to spread the greatest news history has ever heard...

Do you believe God wants to turn the tide?

Remembering who we are

How did we get here in the first place? When Fr James Mallon, a Canadian priest, became pastor of three merged parishes in a brand new church building, he said they couldn't continue to do "business as usual".[5] Continue to do the same things and you get the same results: the decline that led to the merger of three parishes in the first place. He called on his parish to rediscover what *Evangelii Nuntiandi* (*EN*) calls the Church's "deepest identity": the Church exists in order to evangelise (*EN* 14). This is what happens when we forget who we are: we get sick, wither and die.

Do not be afraid

In the Bible, when the Israelites were on the edge of Canaan, the Promised Land, the Lord wanted to show them what an incredible place he had in store for them. He commanded a man from each of the twelve tribes to go and scout out the land (see *Nb* 13:18-20). Forty days later, when the men returned, they recounted how amazing the land was, flowing with milk and honey. Of course, the Israelites wanted to go in immediately and conquer it. But the twelve men's faces were etched with fear. Their armies were not a match for this land's people: "[This] is a country that devours its inhabitants... We felt like grasshoppers, and so we seemed to them" (*Nb* 13:32-33).

When God told the Israelites to scout out the land, they became terrified at the challenge that lay ahead of them. Some of them complained, "Would that we had died in the land of Egypt, or at least that we had died in this wilderness!" (*Nb* 14:2). Some tried to appoint a new leader to take them back into slavery in Egypt. Even slavery would be preferable to the risks involved with what God had put before them.

For some of us in the Church, getting back to our "deepest identity" and therefore changing what we do is like standing on the edge of Canaan: the challenge is so colossal that we would rather do anything than tackle it head on. So adverse are we to risk and change that *death* seems preferable!

Perhaps we knowingly accept that the Church in this country may dwindle to vanishingly small numbers...but we hope we don't live to see it.

Perhaps we are overwhelmed at the change that might be needed...so we simply carry on about our business, faithfully going through the same routines year after year.

Perhaps we park all responsibility at the feet of Church leaders...and so avoid the question on a personal level.

In Scripture, whenever a terrifying situation presents itself, the Lord's response is almost always a resounding *"Do not be afraid!"*

As the Israelites face entering the land of Canaan, the Lord's response through Moses and Aaron is no different:

> The land we went to reconnoitre is a good land, an excellent land. If the Lord is pleased with us, he will lead us into this land and give it to us. It is a land where milk and honey flow. Do not rebel against the Lord. And do not be afraid of the people of this land; we shall gobble them up... *Do not be afraid* of them. (*Nb* 14:7-9)

This is exactly what the Lord seems to be teaching us today:

- Be fully aware of what lies before you.
- Know that I am with you – do not be afraid.

Pope Emeritus Benedict XVI summarised it in these words:

> Dear friends, may no adversity paralyse you. Be afraid neither of the world, nor of the future, nor of your weakness. The Lord has allowed you to live in this moment of history so that, by your faith, his name will continue to resound throughout the world.[6]

> *(Address at World Youth Day, Madrid, 20 August 2011)*

JOURNALLING

- *What is your reaction to the decline in the Church?*
- *Take each line of the quotation from Pope Benedict for your personal prayer:*
    - Is there adversity in your life or vocation that threatens to paralyse you?
    - Do you experience fear in face of the world, the future, or your own weakness?
    - How does it make you feel to know that the Lord has appointed you to live at this moment in history – at this time, in this place?
    - Do you have a sense of the personal mission he has given you to make "his name resound throughout the world"?

There is hope

Nicky Gumbel, vicar of Holy Trinity Brompton church and founder of the Alpha* course, tells the story of a man during World War I who was dying in the trenches. A friend came over to him and asked if there was something he could do for him. The man said no; he knew he was dying. "Is there any message I can take home for you back to England?" asked his friend. And the man replied, "Yes. Please take this message to this man at this address. This is the message: tell him that what he taught me as a child is helping me in my dying moments." So when the friend got back to England, he found the man at that address and told him that what he had

*Alpha is a Protestant evangelical course in the basics of Christianity that originated at Holy Trinity Brompton, an Anglican church. It was popularised in the 1990s by Nicky Gumbel as a tool of evangelisation.

taught this soldier had helped him to die. When he heard this, the man cried, "God forgive me. I gave up teaching Sunday School years ago because I thought what I was doing was having no effect."

Telling people about Jesus – however discouraged we become by the task – always has an effect. Jesus told us to do it, and his power is behind our words. Let us turn now to the message he wants us to share.

What is the Good News?

Some say that the reason we have failed at handing on our faith is because we forgot that Christianity is, above all, a *love story*. We tried to hand on practices and teachings and customs… But this did not make disciples. We forgot the heart of it all.

PONDER

If you had to summarise in one sentence what is at the heart of Christianity, how would you do it?

In his letter, *Evangelii Gaudium (EG)*, Pope Francis summarises the heart of Christianity in a nutshell:

> Jesus Christ loves you; he gave his life to save you; and now he is living at your side every day to enlighten, strengthen and free you. (*EG* 164)

This is what the Church calls the *kerygma*, or the "first proclamation".

Think back to the last time you got some amazing news. The kind of news that made you want to dance around your kitchen as if no one was watching. Maybe it was some medical test results that were clear. Perhaps a job offer. A university place.

Then you go to tell somebody the news. It is so incredible that you cut straight to the chase. You don't waste time with the details, you simply shout out what's happened. "He got the job!" "We're getting married!" "It's a boy!"

In the same way, this is what we mean by the "first proclamation". It is our joyful announcement of this incredible event that has happened.

In Pope Francis's kerygma nutshell in *Evangelii Gaudium* (164), he suggests how you would announce the heart of this amazing story. This is the heart of the matter – we can get to the details later.

Although we can flesh it out with more details, the kerygma should always be up front and centre. Pope Francis reminds us that it can never be "forgotten or replaced by other more important things" (*EG* 164), and that it never "gives way to a supposedly more 'solid' formation" (*EG* 165). "Nothing is more solid, profound, meaningful and wisdom-filled than that initial proclamation." Rather, he says it needs to be announced "at every level and moment" (*EG* 164) – "on the lips of the catechist the first proclamation must ring out over and over" (*EG* 164).

If our catechesis should keep the kerygma – this love story – at the heart of it all, we should spend some time getting to know it. To be effective catechists, we should be able to spell out the kerygma attractively and convincingly. We are therefore going to break it down into five parts.

1) Love that is real, personal, secure

Think back to the amazing news you last received. When we hear something that makes us want to jump up and down, we feel in the euphoria of the news that our life has been blessed, that we are loved. Being loved affects us profoundly. So much do we need to be loved – to experience it, not just to know it theoretically – that Pope St John Paul II went as far as to say, "Man cannot live without love." There are plenty of things we know we cannot live without physically – water, shelter, food, heat – but John Paul II was speaking to the depths of the human heart that he knew so profoundly: we cannot live without love. He expanded his point as follows:

> [Man] remains a being that is incomprehensible for himself, his life is senseless, if love is not revealed to him, if he does not encounter love, if he does not experience it and make it his own, if he does not participate intimately in it.
>
> (*Redemptor Hominis* 10)

Sometimes, it seems we have heard the words "God loves you" so many times that they are emptied of meaning and no longer resonate in our hearts. When that happens, we think of God's love as something vague and impersonal: "Of course, God loves everybody!"

But God is a *passionate* and *personal* lover. Think back to the first time you realised that someone loved you passionately – maybe a first boyfriend or girlfriend who had eyes only for you. How did that love change you? Experiencing love like this for the first time can make reality change from black-and-white to full, dazzling colour. It is a love that expands our hearts. To the people around them, a young couple's fascination with each other can become too much. But the couple themselves? They are blind to everything else; they are set on fire by this love.

Does it sound mad to you that this is the kind of love God the Father loves you with? No, it is not some bland, blanket, fuzzy love that is shared with everyone else. It is a fiery love that *sees* you, *knows* you completely, and is head over heels in love with… *you*. It is personal and it is secure – it will never leave you or let you down. Ever.

2) Even in our sin…

In 2010 there were thirty-three miners in Chile who became trapped underground. They were trapped for sixty-nine days in dark, humid, cramped conditions. They rationed out the little food they had, and each day gathered to pray that God would rescue them. They didn't know whether they would see their families again or get out alive.

When we are in sin, it is like being trapped spiritually in a dark pit, deep underground. Like the impenetrable darkness of being underground, the darkness of sin can overwhelm our soul. We experience self-hatred at what we have done, terrible guilt and shame, and sometimes even despair. In these moments, we feel that we are not worth rescuing, that what we have done is too big, too bad; sin has pushed us once and for all too far from God and all light has been extinguished. We feel alone and unlovable.

There is a line in the Bible that staggers me every time I read it:

> But what proves that God loves us is that Christ died for us while we were still sinners. (*Rm* 5:8)

While we were still sinners. This is what blows my mind. Even in that place of darkness, even in the moment of weakness when I chose the temptation and not the Lord – it is *then* that Christ decided that he loved me so much he didn't want to spend eternity without me. Not when I was at my best, most strong, choosing the right path. No – it was at my *weakest* that God said I was worth dying for. Even in that dark place, God looked on me and felt incomparable love.

3) The great rescuer

In the Holy Land there is a church, near the site of Caiaphas's house in Jerusalem, called the Church of St Peter in Gallicantu. Caiaphas was the high priest who tried Jesus before sending him to Pilate. Beneath the church is a dungeon which is thought to be the cell where Jesus spent the night before being sent to Pilate. It is a tiny cell and could only have been accessed through a shaft from above. It is thought that a prisoner would have been lowered or raised by a rope harness. Pilgrims, as they stand in Jesus's cell, will often pray together from Psalm 40:

> I waited, I waited for the Lord,
> and he stooped down to me;
> he heard my cry.
> He drew me from the deadly pit,
> From the miry clay.
> He set my feet upon a rock,
> And made my footsteps firm.
> (*Ps* 40:1-2)

Think back to the Chilean miners. Incredibly, with much ingenuity and hard work, engineers managed to get a shaft down to the miners. This shaft was so narrow it could fit only one miner at a time. They were lifted, one by one, back to the surface.

Being lowered down into the pit, knowing the brutality of the cross he will face the next day, Jesus shows us he is our rescuer. What is incredible about God's love for us is that he could have just told us we were forgiven. But his mercy for us could not contain itself – he wanted to go himself into the darkness of our pit. He wanted to take all the sin, darkness, shame and pain upon himself. It is like a parent whose child in a faraway country gets into trouble. The parent will move heaven and earth to get out there and bring them back to safety.

The kind of love God shows on the cross is even more crazy, even more passionate than this. God *dies* for us in the flesh. He would do anything to save us from our sin, to bring us back to life and a relationship with him.

How can you possibly be unlovable with a God who would go to such lengths for you? God's love is *real*! God's love is powerful, secure, and it is for you, personally.

4) Death does not have the last word!

What was the last amazing news you received? Good News does not get any better than this. This is it – the news on which our life and faith depends. That, on the third day, Jesus – who had been crucified and buried in a tomb – *rose from the dead*.

As Christians, the news of the Resurrection should blow us away. It is immeasurably *better* than the miners emerging blinking into the daylight and being embraced by their families. It is unimaginably *better* than the news you last received that had you jumping up and down. Death could not handle Jesus and the grave could not hold him! Death has no power over him. This news means that death and sin do not have the last word. They are destroyed – *forever*. He has conquered, he is victorious! We can rejoice – and dance around our kitchen – even now at the joy of our salvation. There are some earth-shattering words that we proclaim on Easter night and that swell our hearts with joy and praise:

This is the night, when Christ broke the prison-bars of death and rose victorious from the underworld.

Though we still experience trouble and temptation, weakness and pain, we really can laugh in their face: ultimately, they will not have the last word. Christ is alive and we will live forever with him.

5) Repent – Believe – Be baptised – Be continuously filled with the Holy Spirit

In the Acts of the Apostles, St Peter preaches the kerygma to the crowd in Jerusalem. Pentecost has just taken place – the Holy Spirit has just been poured out on the Apostles, manifested to all who were gathered there. In Acts 2 you can read Peter's telling of the Gospel message, the kerygma.

As Peter finishes, the Bible tells us that his listeners "were cut to the heart" (v. 37). They approached Peter and the other apostles and asked, "What must we do, brothers?"

PONDER

What would you say, if someone asked how they should respond to this message?

In Acts 2:38, we see Peter's response. "You must repent," he says, "and every one of you must be baptised in the name of Jesus Christ for the forgiveness of your sins, and you will receive the gift of the Holy Spirit."

In his cross and resurrection, Christ has achieved *everything*, once and for all, to reconcile us with God. This is what we call "Redemption". But we have to choose to be redeemed, to be reconciled with God. We respond in four steps.

Step One – Repent   Knowing that our sins have separated us from God, we have to be sorry for them, and desire not to sin again. This is the first step in receiving this free gift of Redemption.

Step Two – Believe   In Romans 10:9, St Paul teaches: "If your lips confess that Jesus is Lord and if you believe in your heart that God raised him from the dead, then you will be saved." God invites us into a life-giving relationship with Jesus Christ – to trust that he is who he said he is, that God raised him from the dead and that through him alone we are saved.

Step Three – Be baptised   These are the words Peter spoke to those who asked what they should do. Baptism is the sign of our being plunged into Jesus's death and raised to new life with him. The mark of original sin is washed away and, instead, the free gift of eternal life is given to us. For someone who is already baptised, there is repentance and renewal of baptismal grace through the Sacrament of Reconciliation.

Repent, believe, be baptised. This is how to follow Christ, how to be a Christian. "And," St Peter adds, "you will receive the gift of the Holy Spirit."

Step Four – Be continuously filled with the Holy Spirit   We are not called to live our Christian lives through our hard work alone. In his summary of the kerygma, Pope Francis wrote that Jesus "is living at your side every day to enlighten, strengthen and free you". He does this through the Holy Spirit.

The real, personal love of God dwells in our hearts after Baptism: "the love of God has been poured into our hearts by the Holy Spirit which has been given us" (*Rm* 5:5). The Holy Spirit is not just a force, a power that fills us. He is a real Person. He indwells us "to enlighten, strengthen and free" us, to shape in each one of us – every day a little more – the image of Jesus.

The Bible, when it speaks of people being filled with the Holy Spirit, uses a Greek verb – plērousthe – that means to be *continuously filled* with the Holy Spirit, to go on being filled (see *Ep* 5:18). This is at the heart of the Christian life – to be filled anew each day with the Holy Spirit. This happens through prayer, reading the Bible, service of others. It happens in a special and particular way when we receive the sacraments.

The kerygma, the Good News of what God has done for us, is the greatest news ever shared in history. More important than anything is that we respond to this great news. God will not save us without us. He wants us to say "yes" to his offer of redemption and to make this life our own.

RECAP

- What are the four steps to take to respond to what God has done for us?
- If you had one minute, how would you tell someone the Gospel message?
- If you had five minutes, how would you tell someone the Gospel message?
- If you had to explain what is meant by the word *kerygma*, what would you say?

CATECHIST TESTIMONY

"In the parish where I work, we proclaim the kerygma each year to the First Communion children and parents at the start of their preparation. We spend a whole day exploring this proclamation of the Good News. The response from the parents has been extraordinary. They said that for the first time they could see the context in which they are bringing their child to the sacraments. It was more than just "coming to Mass"; now they had encountered the whole story."

Sr Veronica Brennan OP, Dominican Sisters of St Joseph

JOURNALLING

- *What most strikes you from this re-telling of the Gospel message, the kerygma?*
- *Which part of the kerygma is God inviting you to know more deeply and personally in your own life?*
- *Which part of the kerygma do you struggle to express in your own words and why? How will you get to know this part more deeply?*

Chapter summary

- Secularisation in the West has radically changed the culture the Church is called to evangelise.

- The Church is called to recall her "deepest identity" – she exists to evangelise – and this identity profoundly shapes catechesis.

- At its heart, Christianity is a love story: God loved us so much he went to unimaginable lengths to show this love and save us from our sin.

- This love story in a nutshell is called the kerygma.

- What God has done will only come alive in us when we respond to him: repent, believe, be baptised and be continuously filled with the Holy Spirit.

LORD, you promised to remain with the Church till the end of time (*Mt* 28:20). We praise you for the fruit the Holy Spirit has brought forth in every age. I offer myself as your instrument to continue making disciples in this moment in history, that more may know the saving message of Jesus Christ. AMEN.

CHAPTER 2:

What Is a Disciple and How Do I Become One?

IN THIS CHAPTER...

• Understand what a disciple is.

• Consider the stages a person moves through in order to become a disciple.

• Reflect on the stories of four individuals as they become disciples of Christ.

For many of us – even Catholics who have been practising our whole lives – we might never have had the opportunity to hear the Gospel message in a way that really penetrates our hearts and – just as important – to respond to it: repent, believe, be baptised, be continuously filled with the Holy Spirit. Or – if we have been baptised as an infant – the other three parts may have been forgotten. It has never even entered our minds to ask those words put to St Peter, "What must we do?" (*Ac* 2:37).

When a person hears the Gospel message and responds to it for the first time, it is a unique moment. It is never the same as another person's experience. In this chapter, we are going to consider how four different people heard the Gospel message for the first time. These four people are fictional, but you may find resonances with your own experience, or with that of others you know.

TOM IS A 19-YEAR-OLD UNIVERSITY STUDENT who has been involved in the diocese's youth ministry throughout his teenage years. He has many friends through this network and feels committed to his Catholic faith. When he started university, he sought out the Catholic chaplaincy and now goes to Mass there most Sundays. Over the years, through World Youth Day, youth groups and other events, he has heard a lot about the Catholic faith. He feels he can explain it to others (although there are some things he is in two minds about himself). But it hasn't sunk in yet – or perhaps he has never really heard – that he could have a relationship with Jesus that is living and personal. He is content with the community and friendships his faith gives him. Deep down, there has always been a small fear that if he opens himself too much to the faith, it will all get too intense. He has met some young people who seem to bring Jesus into everything and he does not want to become like that. He is happy with his faith as it is.

RACHEL IS A 34-YEAR-OLD MOTHER OF TWO. She abandoned her faith when she was in her early twenties, but since having children, she has been keen to return to church and give them the same Catholic upbringing she had. It has been a struggle because her husband, Mike, has no religion. Although she hasn't mentioned it to anyone, Rachel craves some deeper meaning to her life and somehow she thinks faith can give it to her. But taking small children to Mass alone is enormously difficult. That one hour on a Sunday morning is one of the toughest hours of the week. From beginning to end, feelings of stress take over – are the children making too much noise? Am I doing things right? Did that elderly lady just glare at me? The priest's homily doesn't speak much to the craving deep in her heart. She wonders whether all this effort for such little return is worth it.

MARK IS A 45-YEAR-OLD FATHER OF THREE TEENAGE CHILDREN. Two years ago, he and his wife, Joanne, separated. It was an unbearably difficult time. They both knew they had been growing apart for years; they tried marriage counselling, but in the end, Mark had to face up to the reality that Joanne had met somebody else and no longer wanted to make their marriage work. While Joanne stopped going to Mass a while ago, Mark has continued going throughout this messy and difficult period. When the kids are staying with him, they come too, although they complain about it. In the pain and confusion, Mark has found a small amount of solace in the church when it is empty and silent. He likes to pop in and sit in the stillness. He is not even sure if God is there, but he feels peace. Mass on Sundays is much more difficult. Although people know what has happened, very few have reached out to him. They probably don't know what to say. It is much easier for him to sneak in and out and avoid contact outside of the bare minimum. He wonders whether it is in fact necessary to go to Sunday Mass. What does he get out of it?

ANGELA IS 68, JUST RETIRED, WITH FOUR GROWN-UP CHILDREN. Born in the Philippines, she and her husband have spent all their adult lives in the UK. Although she brought her children up in the faith – sent them to Catholic schools and ensured they received the sacraments – none of them now practise. They all lead happy and successful lives, and she is proud of them, although sad that they have not held onto their faith. Now that she is fully retired, Angela and her husband have more time on their hands. There is something nudging Angela to get more involved in her church. Over the years, she has attended Mass every Sunday and has helped at social events when needed. This habit has been drilled into her through her Filipino upbringing. But other than that, she has been too busy to do much more. Now she feels she wants to give more back. Still, there are a few things stopping her. She has never wanted to do anything too visible at church, for example reading at Mass. She would rather stay behind the scenes. But she is concerned that if she starts volunteering more, sooner or later she will be recruited into doing something she doesn't feel comfortable with. She is in two minds.

Becoming an intentional disciple

In 1979, the first year of his pontificate, Pope St John Paul II wrote a short but remarkable document called *Catechesi Tradendae (CT)*; in English, *Catechesis in Our Time*. It is an incredibly insightful and rich document which any catechist should read.

In paragraph 5 of the document, we see one of John Paul II's most insightful comments:

> The definitive aim of catechesis is to put people not only in touch but in communion, in intimacy, with Jesus Christ.

This line sums up the goal of catechesis so pithily that we might find it useful to memorise it by heart.

The goal of catechesis is that a person has *communion* and *intimacy* with Jesus Christ. The name we normally use for someone who has this communion and intimacy with Jesus Christ is a "disciple". The question is, how do we get this communion and intimacy with Jesus? It is the same question the crowds asked Peter in Jerusalem: "What must we do?" (*Ac* 2:37) Or, put another way: How do I become a disciple?

PONDER

Consider the stories of the four people on pages 23-24. From what you know, would you describe any of them as a "disciple" yet? Is there evidence that any of them has "intimacy" or "communion" with Jesus?

In her much-acclaimed 2012 book, *Forming Intentional Disciples*, Sherry Weddell outlines what she calls the "thresholds of conversion" or, in other words, the steps that people take towards becoming a disciple.[7] What follows is a short summary of these thresholds, but as a catechist, you are strongly recommended to read chapters 5-8 in Weddell's book, which describe the thresholds in greater depth. Having a deep understanding of the thresholds, and experience of recognising them in people's lives, is an indispensable skill towards becoming a great catechist.

First threshold – initial trust

Think of someone you know who is aware you are a Christian and accepts it, but would not want to talk about it. They see you as normal and similar to them, so going to church on a Sunday might seem somewhat weird, but it probably isn't "off the chart" extreme. Or perhaps you went to a Catholic school with someone who wasn't a Catholic themselves, but who enjoyed school. Their memories create positive associations with the Church.

For someone who trusts or has a positive association with God, the Church or a Christian believer – but does not yet have an active, personal faith – a "bridge of trust" is in place. As evangelists and catechists, our first task is to find out whether a bridge of trust exists.

If someone is hostile, angry or resentful towards God and/or the Church, a bridge of trust does not exist. Trying to teach them or to speak about God or share the Gospel message with them would be futile or even damaging. Our time would be much better spent building a bridge.

Sometimes it can feel like many of our friendships with people who don't believe are all about building bridges. Evangelising is mostly about friendships – building friendships through love and common interests, and, through prayer and example, asking God for the opportunity to share more with them.

PONDER
Think of the four people profiled previously. Would you say that a "bridge of trust" is in place?

Second threshold – spiritual curiosity

The Argentinian Hollywood actor Eduardo Verástegui has explained how the early stages of his conversion to faith happened. As he was preparing for films, his voice coach would question him. "She would ask me a lot of questions, without judging me, like 'What's your life's purpose?', 'What motivates you to wake up every day?', 'Who do you live for and who do you die for?', 'What does God mean to you?'" Verástegui said during an interview in 2013, "That helped me understand that I was full of contradictions. My faith wasn't the centre of my life. Not because I didn't want it to be, but because I didn't know better."[8]

When a bridge of trust is in place, we can gently move – like Verástegui's voice coach – to arouse curiosity. The Gospels show us that it is far more effective, at this stage in someone's journey, to ask questions than to give answers. After all, it is exactly what Jesus did: "What do you want me to do for you?"; "What do you seek?" (*Mk* 10:51; *Jn* 1:38).

We begin to be aware that someone is curious when they ask half-interested questions. "You went to Mass in your lunch break?" "So what's the deal with eating fish on Fridays?" "How come you're taking your daughter to First Communion classes? Doesn't she already have enough on?" "What's that weird-looking picture in your hallway?"

There's a risk at this point, because our instinct is to jump in and give them the full low-down. Our friend was interested in a quick Google-search answer, and instead we launch in with the no-holds-barred encyclopaedia version. As Weddell says, we drown a teaspoon full of curiosity with gallons of answers.

Part of becoming an effective evangelist and catechist, therefore, is to learn how to match our response to the level of their curiosity. But we can also rouse curiosity. We want our friends to be intrigued that there might be a God who loves them, with whom they can have a personal relationship. We demonstrate this mostly wordlessly through the witness of our lives. But there comes a point when we also use words. We can ask God for an opportunity to say something, for a "divine appointment". The best way to evangelise is to be ourselves and not hide our faith; to say, "Thank God" and "I'll pray for you", to share about Christian events we've been to or how we've experienced answered prayer. Above all, don't theorise (unless your friend invites it). People listen to stories more than ideas, and to witnesses more than teachers. "Modern man listens more willingly to witnesses than to teachers," Pope Paul VI said, "and if he does listen to teachers, it is because they are witnesses" (*EN* 41).

RACHEL'S STORY

The last few Sundays Rachel has been at Mass, she has noticed another young woman who sits as far back as she can, a few rows from her. Maria has a three-year-old girl who has been taking interest in Rachel's young son. There has been an almost immediate affinity between the two mums, the kind of silent encouragement that arises between two people who know they are in the same boat. At the end of Mass one Sunday, as their two toddlers chase each other up and down the path outside, they talk for a little longer than usual. Discovering that they live just streets apart from each other, they decide to meet for coffee during the week.

Rachel and Maria and their children are soon meeting regularly. They rarely speak about church, much more about children, nurseries, what is going on in the local area. Then one morning when they meet, the topic of Mass arises. For Rachel, that longing for deeper purpose in her life won't go away. Is this all there is? The daily grind of juggling children and work and the never-ending list of tasks? As they sit down amid noise and babyccinos, she blurts out, "I must be honest, I don't know why I go to Mass. I don't get anything from it except stress. But you seem peaceful, how do you do it?" "Do I? I find Mass hard too," Maria begins slowly. Then she says, "You know, I think it's more than going to Mass. I think for it all to make sense, you need this relationship with God that touches everything in your life. And you need more than Mass to discover that. I definitely wouldn't have found it by just going to Mass every week." As they carry on talking, Maria invites Rachel to a prayer group that meets in her home every fortnight. "Just come along and meet everyone. I think you'll like it."

TOM'S STORY

There is a girl at Tom's university chaplaincy in whom he's been interested since he first met her at the chaplaincy's curry night. She is pretty, smart and funny. He starts hanging out more at the chaplaincy and building up a stronger circle of friends there. If Emma is at an event, he is sure to be there. Before long, she's showing signs she's interested in him too. One night, the two of them stay up late into the night talking.

One of the things Tom notices is that Emma is more serious about her faith than he is. When she speaks about God, it sounds different – personal, like she knows him. It makes him feel awkward. When she wants to know more about his faith, he changes the conversation. He takes her on a date, and the question of faith comes up again. "My faith isn't like yours," he finally admits. "I don't know...I like to keep it private. I'm happy with it that way." When Emma invites him to a Bible Study, and he declines, he knows there's a problem. He knows somehow this is pushing her away.

For a few weeks, Tom steers clear of the chaplaincy and Emma. He hangs out with his other university mates and throws himself into normal student life – nights out, drinking, other girls. At the back of his mind, he knows that none of these other girls are like Emma. She's fun, she makes him laugh... And it's more than that. There's something special about her. The peace she has, her ability to be herself, is so refreshing. He plucks up the courage and messages her. "What are you up to this weekend?" It turns out Emma is going on a retreat. Of course! He almost laughs out loud. He takes a deep breath. "Is there room for one more?" Hits send. This time it's real... He is putting himself out there. He is open.

Third threshold – openness

Openness is perhaps the hardest threshold. To open yourself to the possibility that all this is real, that a relationship with God is an option, is frightening. It means opening oneself to the possibility of change. It means stepping outside a box you may have created for yourself, a box that helped you make sense of the universe and gave meaning to your life. Only under the influence of grace – the initiative of God – does a person's curiosity translate into openness. Someone on the verge of openness needs people to intercede for them. Becoming open means acknowledging to God that you are open to change, letting go of fear and cynicism, admitting that you may have been wrong. As Weddell comments, "Many who are curious never make this transition."[9]

At this moment, a person is afraid of what they might lose. Will they lose their freedom, their identity, their independence of thought? Pope Benedict XVI gave voice to this fear during the homily of his inaugural Mass as Pope when he said, "If we let Christ enter fully into our lives, if we open ourselves totally to him, are we not afraid that he might take something away from us? Are we not perhaps afraid to give up something significant, something unique, something that makes life so beautiful? Do we not then risk ending up diminished and deprived of our freedom?"

Answering this question, the Holy Father said,

"No! If we let Christ into our lives, we lose nothing, nothing, absolutely nothing of what makes life free, beautiful and great. No! Only in this friendship are the doors of life opened wide. Only in this friendship is the great potential of human existence truly revealed. Only in this friendship do we experience beauty and liberation. And so, today, with great strength and great conviction, on the basis of long personal experience of life, I say to you, dear young people: Do not be afraid of Christ! He takes nothing away, and he gives you everything. When we give ourselves to him, we receive a hundredfold in return. Yes, open, open wide the doors to Christ – and you will find true life."

PONDER

If you were Emma, how would you encourage Tom?

READ

See Sherry Weddell, *Forming Intentional Disciples*, pp. 162-3 about how to help a friend on the verge of openness.

PONDER

In the discipleship profiles so far, are any of the characters yet open to the possibility of a relationship with God?

ANGELA'S STORY

Angela notices in the parish newsletter an advert asking for volunteer help for a new course in the parish. The course is for anyone who wants to discover the basics of Christianity, and each week includes a meal. The coordinator needs volunteers to help cook and serve food. Angela doesn't give a second thought to putting her name down for the first evening to serve food. She loves cooking and is glad she has found a way to give something back.

On the first week of the course, Angela is swept up in the whirlwind of activity in the parish kitchen, but as guests arrive and she serves salad onto one plate after another, her intrigue grows. Some guests are young and have come with friends they know from the parish. Some of them seem nervous, but by the end of the evening, when Angela is serving coffee, there is a lot of laughter and a joyful atmosphere. So intrigued is she, that she volunteers to come back the next week.

One week leads to the next, and before she knows it, the course is over. The volunteers are invited to a celebration party. This time there is no serving or washing up involved and they can enjoy a glass of wine and chat to the guests. Angela and her friend Maggie comment on how happy everyone is. Then, some of the guests share their stories. One after another, Angela hears guests speak about how they discovered something new. They all express it in different ways – "God is real", "I have a relationship with Jesus", "I experienced the Holy Spirit" – and they all have the same joy on their faces. Something stirs in Angela and she doesn't know what it means. At the end of the evening, she turns to Maggie. "Why don't we do the next course?" she says. They both sign up, and Angela starts to feel excitement and trepidation at the same time in the pit of her stomach. Is this really what she wanted on her retirement?

RACHEL'S STORY

The first evening Rachel goes to Maria's house for the prayer group, she feels slightly nervous but is glad of the night off. Mike was happy to look after the kids. As soon as she steps inside, however, she feels relaxed. Everyone else seems completely normal and at a similar stage in life. Maria has prepared fajitas and everyone is digging in. Rachel ends up chatting with two other mums whose children go to the same school as hers. After some introductions, the evening starts with a short talk. Luke, a friend of Maria's husband, shares some of his testimony. From the first moment, Rachel is spellbound. She has never heard anyone speak like this before. There is such honesty in what he is saying – how he'd rejected God for many years, and then, following a retreat he'd attended in his twenties, how God had brought him back. He spoke about how his life was different now: how he prayed every day, how he felt Jesus guiding his life, how he had faced many fears and demons of his past with the help of the Holy Spirit. During the discussion that followed, Rachel barely said a word. She was trying to let what she heard sink in, this way of talking that was so unfamiliar to her.

At the end of the evening, everyone gathers around for worship. Someone gets out a guitar and Rachel can almost feel her toes curl. Is this going to be hideously awkward? She looks at her feet as everyone starts singing. Gradually she relaxes, closes her eyes and lets herself be drawn into the music. It is not as bad as she thought. Then comes a time of silence. In the quietness, trying to ignore how awkward it all feels, Rachel eventually allows a cry in her heart to rise to the surface: "God, if you are real, if you are there, *show me!*" By the end of the evening, there is a feeling of excitement starting to rise in her. One thing she knows is that she is hooked. She hopes Mike won't mind babysitting every fortnight. She has to come back.

Fourth threshold – spiritual seeking

Becoming open to the possibility of a relationship with Christ is a significant step, and can often propel somebody into a full-blown search. No longer are they asking half-hearted, speculative questions. They now know that this relationship is a real possibility, and they wrestle with its potentially life-changing consequences. What will this mean for my life? How will I need to change? Fundamentally, a person who is seeking has begun to encounter Christ and is asking themselves, "Should I give my life to him?"

John Paul II defined the kerygma as:

> the initial ardent proclamation by which a person is one day overwhelmed and brought to the decision to entrust himself to Jesus Christ by faith. (*CT* 25)

A person, through hearing the Good News, is brought to the point where he or she is on the brink of that decision. This is the threshold of spiritual seeking.

TOM'S STORY

The retreat was a weekend of crisis and struggle for Tom. On the first evening, as young adults gathered in worship around the Blessed Sacrament, he stood at the back of the room. He had experienced Adoration many times before, but never in his life had he considered what it meant. Gazing at the white host in the centre of the room, he felt anger and bitterness. What was wrong with the faith that had sustained him up to now? Why wasn't it enough? How was it that

Emma had something so different from him and why did she make it look so easy? All evening he battled with his rage, feeling that he wasn't good enough, hating those young people who seemed so happy and free to praise God.

Then, at one moment of the evening, someone said, "Jesus is truly here, in this room. If you've never spoken to him before, from your heart, now is your chance. He is here and listening to you." At these words, Tom sinks to the ground and looks once more at that little white host. Embarrassingly, tears are pricking his eyes, tears of frustration and desperation. "Jesus, if you are really there and really interested in me, you're going to have to do more than this, because, right now, I don't know if I can believe in you." Almost as soon as he speaks these words in his heart, Tom feels a wave of emotion and heat. It is as though Christ has reached right into his heart and a feeling of overwhelming love fills his body. In an instant, he knows a love he has never experienced before, a love that sees all his self-hatred, fear and anger and loves him anyway. He doesn't know how long he stays there, flooding the floor around him in tears. Later, as the evening programme finishes, he gazes in the silence at Christ, overwhelmed with love for him, knowing that from this day forward he has a friend like no other, and feeling like he could stay sitting in that spot for eternity.

Coming back to university from the retreat, everything has changed in Tom's heart. He sees the whole world differently. He sees Emma differently. She is as pretty and funny as ever, but now someone else has the most important place. He is spending more time watching YouTube clips and reading about Christ than he is looking for opportunities to hang out with Emma. Now he is desperate to go to the Bible Study in the chaplaincy, more to answer his own questions than to spend time with her. But they stay up late afterwards talking. He is connecting with her on a new level and he can tell how happy it makes her. But what makes him happiest is his discovery of this new friendship with Christ; and whatever happens, whether he and Emma stay together or not, this is all that matters.

MARK'S STORY

Most days Mark is able to keep the depression and hopelessness he feels about his failed marriage at bay. Work is busy and he throws himself into it as a coping mechanism. But one evening, the feeling of loss and failure overwhelms him. Deep down, he feels he is not only a failed husband and father, but a failed Catholic too. Never did he imagine that his own marriage would end in separation. What options are left to him now? What can the future possibly hold? He heads to church as he always does when he feels moments of wretchedness like this. But today as he walks through the doors, he wonders what the point is. There is a moment when he almost turns away, but something urges him through the door. He heads towards the normal spot where he likes to sit in the chapel of St Joseph. Today is different. Something makes him kneel at the rail before the small altar and, pouring out his sorrow, he begs St Joseph for help. His heart seems to cry, "I am totally lost, completely alone. Everything I hoped for is gone." As time goes on, he is aware that a quiet but unmistakable peace has overtaken him; in a strange way it feels like he is gently being held, that somehow, mysteriously, he is not completely alone.

He stays there a long time, in what feels like a spiritual embrace. He has the strange sensation that he is resting his head on Christ. Eventually, he lifts his head and though the sorrow is still present, Mark feels he is still being held by a strong, utterly secure love. As he stands up to leave, some words come into his mind: "Leave all your sins at the Cross." Where did they come from? He is unsure, but they are clear as day. He needs to go to Confession.

In the next week, Mark goes to Confession and feels like he is confessing his sins for the first time in his life. He withholds nothing, knowing that this love he experienced upholds him. It is an emotional encounter and he is touched by the priest's compassion and wise advice. They continue talking after his Confession has finished, and the priest tells him to keep in touch.

Over the next few months, Mark finds himself going regularly to speak with Fr David. Occasionally they meet for a drink together, and one evening they meet for dinner with other friends of Fr David. For Mark, a whole new world begins to open up. With these new friends he can ask questions about the Catholic faith he has never even thought about before, and they give him knowledgeable responses. They don't think he is ignorant for asking such basic questions; they are charitable and wise. As Mark's knowledge of the faith grows, he realises how much he has been missing out. He now goes to Mass with a deeper understanding of what is happening, he ensures he goes to Confession regularly and he starts exploring new ways to pray. Before long, it feels like his life has purpose, the pain in his heart begins to dull, and for the first time ever, he dares to believe that God might be guiding his life.

Fifth threshold – intentional discipleship

It is difficult to remain seeking forever. Weddell writes, "We might say, 'I can't *not* do this!' The point is that a human being reaches the moment where – with complete freedom – she chooses to sell all she has to purchase the Pearl of Great Price and become a follower of Christ (see *Mt* 13:45-46)."[10]

RACHEL'S STORY

Wednesday nights at Maria's, every two weeks, are becoming Rachel's lifeline. She would move heaven and earth not to miss one of these nights, and luckily, Mike is obliging. He says she seems happier. Each week, Rachel listens intently to someone from the prayer group share either their testimony or how they live their faith in everyday life. Gradually, Rachel builds up the confidence to express her own thoughts and ask questions. She soaks up what people share with her like a sponge. She has never desired something so much in her life. She too wants that kind of connection with God that will sustain her from day to day. She tries speaking to God through the day. She doesn't feel as if God responds to her and she feels downhearted, but then thinks, "If these people can experience God, so can I."

One evening, the talk is about the Holy Spirit. In the time of praise that follows, Rachel feels a strong desire to be filled with the Holy Spirit. She knows that the Holy Spirit already fills her through her Baptism and Confirmation, but she is desperate for the Holy Spirit to flood her life. Everyone begins to pray with each other in twos and threes, and two of the prayer group members offer to pray with Rachel. She holds out her hands as they pray, "Come, Holy Spirit." She stands there feeling nothing but a sense of peace. She thought perhaps she would feel something more than that, but the peace is real and she doesn't mind. Incredibly, over the next week, she begins to feel more positive about her life. She wakes up in the morning feeling that God is with her. She finds herself speaking in her heart to him throughout the day and feels like she's somehow a little girl chatting to her Father. She finds she has more patience with her children. She asks God for strength when she feels weak or exhausted or frustrated. Things are changing.

ANGELA'S STORY

Although full of trepidation on the first evening, Angela's experience of the course has been unlike anything she has done before. She had always understood what her faith required of her. But here she is experiencing something new. She can barely put it into words, but what keeps coming back to her is that God is a *person*. She loves listening to the other people in her group each week and they soon become firm friends. There is a lot of laughter. When they go on a weekend away towards the end of the course, she reflects that there has been a quiet, but undeniable, shift in her life. She understands that God sees everything in her life, not as a demanding judge, but as a doting Father. This awareness has lifted years off her. She feels lighter, happier and freer. Her husband Joe recognises a difference; he says she laughs more. He asks if he can do the course too.

When the course finishes, Angela immediately signs up for a Bible Study in the parish. She is ravenous to understand more about this God who loves her. The Bible Study is led by a Sister in the parish, and Angela feels as if she is hearing everything with new ears. At one time, she would have found all this quite dull and tedious, part of the necessary drudgery that her faith demanded. Now, she can't hear enough. Some days it still feels unbelievable that God really could love her so much.

PONDER

Take each of the four characters. At which points in their stories would you guess they are moving through different thresholds? In the margin of each story, write the thresholds you identify – trust, curiosity, openness, seeking, intentional discipleship.

Think about your own life of following Christ. Use the diagram on p. 35 to plot different moments of your life when you passed through different thresholds. It is important to remember that a person rarely crosses these thresholds in a linear fashion. We can move both forwards and backwards in the spiritual life, as well as come to a standstill. Take this diagram to prayer to reflect on where you are today, and what invitation God is extending to you.

Acknowledgement: Sherry Weddell/Catherine of Siena Institute. Used with permission.

Non-believing,
non-trusting

TRUST – THRESHOLD 1

CURIOSITY – THRESHOLD 2

OPENNESS – THRESHOLD 3

SEEKING – THRESHOLD 4

INTENTIONAL DISCIPLESHIP

Baptism

CHRIST

JOURNALLING

*Read Matthew 4:18-22; "And they left their nets at once and followed him."
Have you dropped your own nets to follow Christ? If you feel you haven't made
a personal, intentional commitment to Christ, feel free to pray the following
prayer, or a similar one in your own words. You may also want to take the
opportunity to receive the Sacrament of Reconciliation.*

LORD JESUS, I believe that you have come to show us
the face of the Father.

I believe that you want to have a personal and intimate
relationship with me.

I am sorry for all I have done to reject you and separate
myself from you.

I desire to enter into your love and live my life in
communion with you. AMEN.

A beginning disciple

FOCUS (the US-based Fellowship of Catholic University Students) developed the Discipleship Roadmap to show the stages a person moves through on becoming a disciple. There are certain characteristics we can detect in a person who is beginning to make an intentional decision to follow Jesus as his disciple. The characteristics we shall consider are based on the FOCUS resource.[11]

PONDER

Which of the following characteristics can you spot in the stories of Tom, Rachel, Mark and Angela so far?

Attitude of a Disciple	Tom	Rachel	Mark	Angela
Change of attitude towards Jesus Christ and the Church he established (favourable) (*Rm* 10:8-10)				
Change of attitude towards sin (unfavourable) (*1 Jn* 1:5-9)				
Has made a verbal profession of commitment to Jesus Christ to others (*Mk* 5:18-20)				
Desires to grow spiritually (*Ph* 4:8)				
Has received the sacraments of initiation or has gone to Confession if already a Catholic (*Ac* 2:37-38)				

Chapter summary

- A disciple is someone who has "intimacy" and "communion" with Jesus.

- We can identify certain spiritual stages a person moves through on the way to making an intentional and conscious decision to follow Christ in the context of his Church.

- This is not a linear journey, and every person's conversion is unique, but as evangelists we need to have an awareness of the thresholds, and how we can best help a person at each stage.

JESUS, I desire intimacy and communion with you. I wish to deepen my decision to be your disciple. Give me a passion not just to follow you, but to do everything in my power to help others come to know and follow you. AMEN.

CHAPTER 3:

What Is Catechesis?

IN THIS CHAPTER…

• Consider the nature and purpose of catechesis within the context of evangelisation.

• Understand what is meant by the "pedagogy of God".

• Understand the role of the catechist as agent of the Church who hands on what he or she has received.

• Consider what it means for catechesis to be kerygmatic.

When John Paul II described the definitive aim of catechesis, he wrote that it had to put people not only in touch with Jesus, but in "intimacy" and "communion" with him. In all four stories we heard, each of the characters were beginning to experience intimacy and communion with Jesus, and were embarking upon the journey of a disciple. None of them had received formal catechesis, although most had long conversations with friends with whom they discussed their questions.

PONDER

If you had to define catechesis, what would you write?

The word "catechesis" translates the Greek word *katechein* (to echo). It is a rare word, hardly known in the religious vocabulary of Judaism, but St Paul uses it frequently in his New Testament letters to describe giving instruction concerning the content of the faith. The more common Greek word was *didaskein* (to teach) and this is also used, but *katechein* is used as a technical term for Christian instruction. St Paul seems to be emphasising that handing on the Gospel is a very particular kind of instruction, unlike any other kind of teaching. (Look up *Lk* 1:4; *Ac* 18:25; *Rm* 2:18; *1 Co* 14:19 for examples of *katechein* being used in the New Testament.)[12]

Clearly, catechesis is not just teaching knowledge, although it does include that. John Paul II reveals well what *katechein* means in these words:

> Catechesis aims therefore at developing understanding of the mystery of Christ in the light of God's word, so that the whole of a person's humanity is impregnated by that word. Changed by the working of grace into a new creature, the Christian thus sets himself to follow Christ and learns more and more within the Church to think like Him, to judge like Him, to act in conformity with His commandments, and to hope as He invites us to. (*CT* 20)

As you were reading the last chapter, you may have wondered: Is all this more than I bargained for? All I'm doing is preparing children for First Communion. When I was young, we just learnt what was happening at Mass. Isn't this stuff on discipleship a bit too much?

In the stories of the four people described above, it is clear that discovering their faith was not a process of learning some facts that left their lives mostly unchanged. For each of them, in four very different ways, their encounter with Jesus started to change them. John Paul II (*CT* 20) suggests that this change must go even further. The aim of the Christian life is that "the whole of a person's humanity is impregnated by [the light of God's] word" and that, through the working of grace, a person is "changed ...into a new creature".

Ponder these words. This is huge. It means the transformation of your being.

If it seems a bit radical to you, you are surely not alone. It would be much easier to take a textbook and teach children facts about their faith. This is good in itself, but it can't end there. God desires much more than this. He wants to see our lives change.

But – you might be asking – I signed up to be a catechist, not an evangelist! Surely these two are not the same thing?

Since the Second Vatican Council in the 1960s, successive popes called on the Church to shift all her activities to become completely mission-oriented. When he opened the Council in 1962, Pope John XXIII said, "In order to respond to the Saviour's command the whole Church must be put on a missionary footing!" Everything we do should be marked by our identity, which is to evangelise, to share the Good News. Evangelisation describes the very identity of the Church, and includes all her activity – including catechesis. John Paul II emphasised this once again in 1983 when he wrote:

> The proclamation of the Word of God [which includes catechesis] has Christian conversion as its aim: a complete and sincere adherence to Christ and his Gospel through faith... Conversion means accepting, by a personal decision, the saving sovereignty of Christ and becoming his disciple. (*Redemptoris Missio* 46)

Let's break this down:

- The aim of catechesis is conversion.

- Conversion involves a personal decision to accept Christ and his salvation.

- This means becoming Christ's disciple.

Think back to the girl in Chapter 1 who wasn't sure she believed in God. For her, all the catechesis she received did not achieve its aim. There may have been a whole host of reasons why it failed, but it was important for us as a team to be honest about it.

PONDER

Think about catechesis in your parish. To what extent does it bring about and deepen conversion in people? To what extent do people become disciples of Christ thanks to catechesis they receive?

Where does catechesis fit?

Pope Paul VI understood that evangelisation is a "complex, rich and dynamic reality" (*EN* 17). If you think of the ways that the four people were brought into a relationship with God, many different factors were involved: friendship, witness, personal and corporate prayer, service, discussion. Catechesis is just one element – an essential "moment" – in the whole process of evangelisation (*General Directory for Catechesis* 63).

Importantly, it is "distinct from the primary proclamation of the Gospel" (*CT* 19). When we unpacked the kerygma, we said this was the "first" or "primary" proclamation of the Good News – the quick, breathless message or announcement. The details

would come later. Catechesis is that "moment" when the details are given. Imagine your best friend excitedly messages you to say that she's getting married. It is only later, when you sit down with a coffee, that she tells you all the details – how the day unfolded, how her fiancé proposed, her reactions, feelings and thoughts – all the details that you want to know when you love someone.

And here is the crunch. We only care about the details of someone's marriage proposal or job offer or new house when we love them. If someone at work with whom you are barely acquainted starts waxing lyrical about the details of her new home, you soon find yourself pretty bored, hoping she moves swiftly on to somebody else.

This is why a relationship with God is needed before any of the details can be given. The 14-year-old girl in my Confirmation class had been hearing the details all year, without any sense of a personal connection with God. It is likely that she had spent the whole year feeling fairly bored.

The *General Directory for Catechesis* expresses it like this:

> Frequently, many who present themselves for catechesis truly require genuine conversion. Because of this the Church usually desires that the first stage in the catechetical process be dedicated to ensuring conversion." (*GDC* 62)

Those of us with many years of giving catechesis behind us are likely to be nodding sagely at this quotation. People come asking for all the details about someone they have never met and don't have too much interest in. Imagine Tom signed up for catechesis before his conversion, or Rachel, Mark or Angela. Imagine they arrived at a class where a catechist enthusiastically unpacked the doctrine of the Trinity. Maybe it would have interested them on some level. But imagine they dropped in *after* the conversion they had experienced, hungry to know more. They would have eagerly absorbed the catechist's words, because knowing God about whom he or she was speaking makes all the difference. Now they want to know everything about him.

Catechesis "promotes and matures initial conversion, educates the convert in the faith and incorporates him into the Christian community" (*GDC* 61). "Only by starting with conversion…can catechesis, strictly speaking, fulfil its proper task of education in the faith" (*GDC* 62).

If catechesis is one "moment" of evangelisation, the diagram below shows what the other "moments" are. If we have heard the Gospel message and responded to it, as Jesus's disciple, we are in ongoing need – until the day we die – of evangelisation.

PONDER

Think of the catechesis in your parish.
- *At what stage is the kerygma proclaimed? How is it proclaimed?*
- *How do you know how people are responding to it?*
- *Do you have a way of gauging whether people are experiencing a conversion of heart and growing in their desire to become a disciple?*
- *What obstacles are there in your current programme to making disciples?*

CATECHIST TESTIMONY

"We might assume that catechumens have heard the Gospel proclaimed elsewhere, and that our job as catechists is simply to explain, not to preach or proclaim. But people come to RCIA [Rite of Christian Initiation of Adults] for all different reasons, some because they have indeed heard the Gospel, but others come because they are searching for meaning and consolation that the world cannot give, or simply because they know a Catholic who they admire. Some show up for all the wrong reasons – to get their children into Catholic school, or to be able to have the church wedding a fiancé wants – but this is all the more reason to proclaim the Gospel message clearly and insistently. It's so easy to become preoccupied with making the Faith intellectually respectable, and to turn RCIA into a sort of extended Q&A, but there is no point in the explanation without the Gospel message. If a catechumen has not heard the Good News that God became man to save him from his sins, then all the detailed theology in the world will not make him a disciple. We don't teach the Gospel simply because it is interesting, we teach it because it is life-changing, indeed world-changing."

Victoria Seed, Holy Trinity and St Augustine of Canterbury Catholic Church, Baldock

God takes the initiative

Within the whole process of evangelisation, the aim of catechesis is to be the teaching and maturation stage, that is to say, the period in which the Christian, having accepted by faith the person of Jesus Christ as the one Lord and having given Him complete adherence by sincere conversion of heart, endeavours to know better this Jesus to whom he has entrusted himself. (*CT 20*)

RACHEL'S STORY

She's been going to the prayer group for over a year. It is amazing how much her life has changed. Every day Rachel makes sure she has some quiet time, at least ten minutes of prayer where she tries to read the Bible. It sounds crazy to say it, but God has become her greatest friend, one who knows her even more deeply than she knows herself. But she is aware that her understanding is lacking. There are so many questions she has about the Mass, about Scripture and the Church's teaching, and at the prayer group there is not enough time to ask all her questions. What's more, daily life is a struggle to keep on top of everything. Prayer group friends recommend books, podcasts, articles, but she hasn't found time for any of it.

When her son is old enough to prepare for First Communion, Rachel is delighted when she hears that the parish programme also includes the parents. Maybe this is her chance to learn more. Every month, while the children have their own session, the parents take part in a catechetical session which covers the basics. The way the priest and the lay catechist explain different parts of the faith sets Rachel's heart on fire. Pieces are beginning to click together. When she has her time of prayer each morning, she finds herself reflecting more on what she has heard and reading lines from the *Compendium of the Catechism* they have been given. This knowledge opens her to a deeper awareness of the presence of the Holy Spirit in her life. She also realises that there are some areas of her life she needs to change, and she wants to respond.

The *Catechism of the Catholic Church* tells us:

> Catechesis for the "newness of life" (*Rm* 6:4) in [Christ] should be: – a *catechesis of the Holy Spirit*, the interior Master of life according to Christ, a gentle guest and friend who inspires, guides, corrects, and strengthens this life. (*CCC* 1697)

The most encouraging reality for the catechist is that the Holy Spirit is the interior teacher. When Rachel turned up for catechesis in her parish, it is likely that the priest and catechist had little idea of her conversion. Yet, the Holy Spirit had been at work in her soul for a long time before she even heard their teaching.

This is an extremely significant point for catechesis. The goal of God's revelation of himself and of everything he has done for us is our salvation. We know that "God never ceases to draw man to himself" (*CCC* 27). We can say that each person's life is a story of how God is seeking out that person. "He liberates the person from the bonds of evil and attracts him to himself by bonds of love. He causes the person to grow progressively and patiently towards the maturity of a free son, faithful and obedient to his word" (*GDC* 139). The Church calls this the "pedagogy of God" (sometimes the "divine pedagogy"). By pedagogy, we normally understand "the theory and practice of teaching". When we speak of God's pedagogy, we are referring to how he teaches us, but the concept is wider than this. The pedagogy of God refers both to:

- how God has revealed himself in history, pre-eminently in Christ, and

- how he continues to teach, guide and develop each person as his disciple, through the gift of the Holy Spirit.

Read more in *GDC* 137-147.

In the salvation of each person, God does all the heavy lifting. *GDC* speaks about the "dialogue of salvation" that takes place between God and each person in the context of the divine pedagogy. ("Dialogue of salvation" is a great phrase because it reminds us that, although Christ has done *everything* for us to be saved, our response is still needed.) It has big implications for catechesis. If this is the work that God is doing already, even before we begin catechesis, it makes a big impact on how we see our role.

PONDER

Make a note for yourself: what are the implications for catechesis?

GDC 143 spells out what the impact is as follows:

- That God's initiative precedes our work.

- That we step into the work of revelation and salvation already happening in a person's life.

- That our catechesis should both *serve* and *be inspired by* God's own pedagogy.

In Part 3, we will come back to this third point – how catechesis learns from and imitates the divine pedagogy. But for the moment let's stay with the idea that catechesis plays a significant part in God's own pedagogy.

Catechesis is "active pedagogy in the faith" (*GDC* 144); in other words, *it is one of the main tools God uses as part of his own pedagogy.* Think of this: when you are teaching, God uses it as one of the main ways he draws a person to himself, teaches, guides and develops them.

While God's salvific action is distinguished from our teaching, "the salvific action of God" and "the pedagogical action of man" (*GDC* 144) work together. "The wonderful dialogue that God undertakes with every person becomes [the] inspiration and norm [of catechesis]" (*GDC* 144). "Truly, to help a person to encounter God, which is the task of the catechist, means to emphasise above all the relationship that the person has with God so that he can make it his own and allow himself to be guided by God" (*GDC* 139).

Of course, Rachel is completely unaware of all this when she is at the parents' catechesis. Perhaps the session begins with music and prayer and she opens her heart to the Holy Spirit. Maybe another parent shares a testimony of how God is at work in her life, which deepens Rachel's commitment to seek God every day. When the Scripture is read and explained passionately and authoritatively, a light bulb goes on in her mind. She understands something that has not been clear to her before. Through the teaching, she begins to realise that parts of her life need to change. At the end of the session, during a time of silent prayer in the church, she speaks intimately to God and makes a resolution to begin making these changes.

PONDER
How does what you have read above change how you see catechesis?

"How are they to believe in him of whom they have never heard? And how are they to hear without a preacher?" (*Rm* 10:14)

How we teach is significant given that we are cooperating with God's own work in a person's life. We will come back to the question of 'how' in Part 3. But *what* we teach is equally important.

One simple definition of catechesis, penned by Mgr Francis D Kelly, is: "Catechesis is the transmission of God's Word to invite people to personal faith."[13] God's Word is something that is not human knowledge, "even of the highest kind" (*CT* 58). It is revelation from God, *not* what we know through our own experience or insights.

> By natural reason man can know God with certainty, on the basis of his works. But there is another order of knowledge, which man cannot possibly arrive at by his own powers: the order of divine Revelation. Through an utterly free decision, God has revealed himself and given himself to man. This he does by revealing the mystery, his plan of loving goodness, formed from all eternity in Christ, for the benefit of all men. God has fully revealed this plan by sending us his beloved Son, our Lord Jesus Christ, and the Holy Spirit. (*CCC* 50)

Sometimes, when I have given catechesis on Revelation or on the Blessed Trinity to young people, I start with a short activity. I invite everyone to write on a piece of paper a fact about themselves that no one else in the room knows. We gather in the papers, then hand them back out. Each person reads the fact they received and guesses which person the fact applies to. The activity illustrates that, unless the person had revealed this fact about themselves, we would not know it. Similarly with God's revelation: if he had not revealed himself to us – particularly in Jesus – we would not know him.

Dr Petroc Willey discusses how we can think of catechesis as "unveiling". In 2 Corinthians 3, St Paul uses this imagery. The old covenant is veiled, it cannot be understood, without Christ, "because only through Christ is [the veil] taken away" (*2 Co* 3:14). St Paul uses the idea of the veil to mean that something cannot be understood, yet, "when a man turns to the Lord the veil is removed" (v. 16). It is with "unveiled faces" that we behold God's glory (v. 18). Unveiling can be a powerful image for catechesis.[14]

I realised this powerfully once as an RCIA catechist. One of the young women preparing to be baptised (let's call her Rebecca) had experienced a completely unexpected but life-changing conversion when she stumbled across World Youth Day while in Madrid in 2011. Hearing truths about the Catholic faith for the first time during the RCIA sessions when she came back home to England, she drank up this new knowledge thirstily, and her life began to change. She would get up early each morning to pray the Rosary, and every part of her new life began to be touched by her new-found faith.

There was one area that was still untouched, however. Rebecca had lived with her boyfriend for several years and so far, in the whirlwind of her new life, she had not yet heard that the authentic place for sex was within the covenant of marriage. I still vividly remember the lunch we had together where the topic came up. By now we were good friends, and I knew it was time to broach the issue. She took it exceedingly well, and immediately said she wanted to live her life according to what God wanted. For her, it was a kind of "unveiling" where she understood the truth about this area of her life. We agreed to pray together for nine days while she worked out a plan of action. Within a few weeks, she had moved out from where she had been living with her boyfriend, into a spare bedroom in her sponsor's house. Today, several years later, Rebecca is a mature disciple of Christ, on fire with her faith, and spreading that passion to those who meet her.

The Holy Spirit is the "gentle guest and friend who inspires, guides, corrects, and strengthens this life" (*CCC* 1697), but he needs our courage, cooperation and witness.

"I hand over to you what I received"

READ

Look up two passages of Scripture: 1 Corinthians 15:3-5 and 1 Corinthians 11:23-24.

In 1 Corinthians 15, Paul is preaching the central Gospel message, the kerygma. In 1 Corinthians 11, he is sharing with the Corinthians the form of the Eucharist. In both, he uses similar phrases to transmit them. He says, "I delivered [or handed over] to you...what I had received."

In using this phrase, St Paul emphasises "These are not my own thoughts or ideas. This is what I have received." Catechesis is an ecclesial activity. As a catechist, you are an "agent" of the Church, handing down faithfully what you have received: catechesis is "a question of communicating God's Revelation in its entirety" (*CT* 58).

TOM'S STORY

During the holidays, Tom takes the opportunity to attend a summer school. It is on the Theology of the Body, the teaching of John Paul II on human love in God's plan. It is the kind of thing he would have run a mile from this time last year, but it is something Emma has raved about a few times. He decides he needs to get clued up, and signs up for the school. From the first lecture he is captivated. The lecturer's depth of knowledge – his understanding of Scripture, philosophy, theology, anthropology – blows his mind. He has never heard anyone teach with such authority before. Over the next few days, he scribbles prolifically, reads more Scripture than ever before, and finds himself unafraid in the open environment to ask challenging questions.

What sticks with him over the week – what hits him with remorse and shame – is how arrogant he has been in his views. Despite his years of experience in the Church, he has always held his own views when it comes to relationships and sexuality. He has always believed that if two people really love each other and are committed to each other, they should be able to have sex. Now he hears for the first time about the language of the body, and the covenant of marriage, and it all makes sense why sex should be exclusively for marriage. On a host of other questions, too, Tom's own views are one by one gently dismantled.

One day he challenges the lecturer, "But what about you personally? What if your personal view is not in line with the Church's?" The lecturer's response strikes him with its humility. He answers that if he believes in Christ, then he also believes the Church that is wedded to Christ, and to which Christ has given all his authority. When you consider the centuries of Tradition, the great minds and the Saints that have guarded and unfolded the Deposit of Faith, what is his small intellect in comparison? He adds that he does sometimes struggle with some of the Church's teachings, but that it is important for him to wrestle personally with God, asking the advice of others, and never to publically criticise the Church's teaching.

It is this response more than anything else he has heard that challenges Tom, and over the week, he realises his intellectual outlook and worldview is shifting in a way he never thought possible.

Kerygmatic catechesis

PONDER

We have already encountered the word "kerygma". Based on your knowledge of this, what do you think is meant by "kerygmatic catechesis"?

Back in Chapter 1, we explored what Pope Francis had to say about the place of the kerygma – the Gospel message – in catechesis. For a person to first believe in Jesus Christ and what he has done for them, they need to hear the message of the Gospel, the "first proclamation". It is this message that is at the heart of Christianity, and the message to which we continually return. It never "gives way to a supposedly more 'solid' formation" (*EG* 165). "Nothing is more solid, profound, meaningful and wisdom-filled than that initial proclamation."

In *CT* 25, John Paul II unpacks this point further:

> Through catechesis the Gospel kerygma…is gradually deepened, developed in its implicit consequences, explained in language that includes an appeal to reason, and channelled towards Christian practice in the Church and the world. All this is no less evangelical than the kerygma, in spite of what is said by certain people who consider that catechesis necessarily rationalises, dries up and eventually kills all that is living, spontaneous and vibrant in the kerygma. The truths studied in catechesis are the same truths that touched the person's heart when he heard them for the first time. Far from blunting or exhausting them, the fact of knowing them better should make them even more challenging and decisive for one's life.

John Paul II's words are rather strong. It is not the case, he says, that once someone has heard and responded to the Gospel message we can get on with teaching the more rational, solid and heady content. No – catechesis is not meant to "rationalise, dry up or…kill all that is living, spontaneous and vibrant in the kerygma." The amazing revelation that God loves, died in the flesh and rose again for someone – which "overwhelmed" them and brought them to the decision to entrust themselves to Jesus – these are the same truths that catechesis unveils more vividly.

This has two big implications for catechesis:

• **What we teach (content):** Every doctrine we teach – whether it be the Eucharist, Our Lady, Purgatory or the priesthood – should be taught in relation to the kerygma. The kerygma should be proclaimed in *every* catechetical session. It is a very useful exercise as a catechist to take any doctrine – perhaps choose one from the *Catechism of the Catholic Church* at random – and explain it in relation to the kerygma.

• **How we teach (method):** We are most effective catechists when we are *witnesses*. It means our teaching flows from our own experience of the joy of salvation. Another useful exercise is to consider how you would teach a doctrine in relation to your own testimony. This makes it personal and real for the listeners, but most importantly, it ensures the catechesis stays kerygmatic – tied to your own testimony of conversion. Above all, joy and enthusiasm should mark our catechesis: "an evangeliser must never look like someone who has just come back from a funeral!" (*EG* 10)

ANGELA'S STORY

There are two things that continue to deepen Angela's faith. One is the Bible Study with Sr Teresa. Every week, she seems to come back to the heart of it all once again. Faith is a love story and God is relentlessly pursuing us. The other is that her husband, Joe, has now finished his course and it has had a profound impact on his life. He prays every day, early in the morning, and one day he urges her to join him. This involves a sacrifice because she enjoys sleeping a little later, but she is determined to begin this habit.

The other change in Joe is his desire to serve. What has happened to the man who had wanted to spend his retirement on the golf course? Of course, he still gets out there a couple of times a week. But now he has made another commitment: to help in the soup kitchen near their house every Friday. "God has given us so much, Angela," he says, "and I feel like we've wasted a lot of time."

A growing disciple[15]

When a person commits to living their life as a disciple, they need catechesis in order to grow. Which of the following characteristics can you spot in the stories of Tom, Rachel, Mark and Angela so far?

Attitude of a Disciple	Tom	Rachel	Mark	Angela & Joe
Has developed a heart for God that motivates his/her attitudes and actions				
Is willing to make any sacrifices to grow, even change his/her schedule				
Observable changes in attitudes and actions can be seen				
Consistent in continually growing in the basic habits of the Christian life, including but not limited to:				
• Seeking interior growth through daily prayer with Scriptural and spiritual reading (*Jn* 1:1-18; *Ep* 6:18)				
• Growing in sanctification through the reception of the sacraments (*Ac* 2:42)				
• Building character through the virtues and the Beatitudes (*Mt* 5:1-16)				
• Accepting suffering and uses it to unite him/her to Christ (*Col* 1:24)				
• Practising the spiritual and corporal works of mercy (*Mt* 25:31-46)				
• Being open to the Holy Spirit (*Jn* 16:7; 12-13)				

Chapter summary

- "Catechesis is the transmission of God's Word to invite people to personal faith." (Mgr FD Kelly)

- Catechesis is a distinctive "moment" in the process of evangelisation (*GDC* 63) where a person understands more deeply the mystery of Christ to whom they have entrusted themselves. It is the "teaching and maturation stage" of becoming a disciple of Christ (*CT* 20).

- The primary teacher in catechesis is the Holy Spirit (*CCC* 1697), the One who draws each person, through countless ways, into the life of God (*CCC* 27).

- The catechist is the agent used by God to teach everything that has been revealed and entrusted to the Church (*CT* 58). The catechist is aware of serving the pedagogy of God (*GDC* 143).

- Catechesis does not replace but deepens and develops a person's response to the kerygma (*CT* 25) and is therefore kerygmatic in its nature.

LORD, I love all that you have revealed of yourself in your Word, and I long to know it more deeply. Transform me by your Word, so that I may more effectively transmit it to others. AMEN.

CHAPTER 4:

The Mission of the Catechist

> The Church awakens and discerns this divine vocation and confers the mission to catechise. The Lord Jesus invites men and women, in a special way, to follow him, teacher and formator of disciples. This personal call of Jesus Christ and its relationship to him are the true moving forces of catechetical activity. (*GDC* 231)

By now, the reality should be dawning on you that good catechesis does not depend on the latest programme or the most cutting-edge online series. No, good catechesis is down to the Holy Spirit and *you*. Christ intended the Good News to be handed on person to person. He didn't write a book or make a film series; he gathered twelve disciples.

So far, we have seen that when people arrive for catechesis:

• They should hear the kerygma, attractively proclaimed, over and over.

• They should have an opportunity to respond – repent, believe, be baptised (or receive Reconciliation) and be continuously filled with the Holy Spirit.

• The catechist creates conditions for them to encounter Jesus, aware that God has taken the initiative.

• They should hear the teaching handed down by the Church through the centuries, not the catechist's own opinions.

IN THIS CHAPTER...

• Consider the human and spiritual qualities of an effective catechist.

• Reflect on your own calling to be a catechist and how God has worked in your life.

• Consider how to deepen your discipleship especially through a spiritual plan of life.

PONDER

If this is what good catechesis looks like, what qualities would an effective catechist need to develop? List both human and spiritual qualities.

If good catechesis depends on the Holy Spirit and you, then *you* are the most important resource to invest in. Christ desires that your whole life and manner of being, the way you teach and communicate, gives witness to him. This vocation is about far more than teaching some facts. It is about drawing people into a living relationship with Christ. It is impossible to do this unless you know him personally:

> The first and essential object of catechesis is, of course, the person of Jesus of Nazareth... The catechists' concern should be to transmit, through their teaching and behaviour, the doctrine and life of Christ. Their mode of being and of working should depend entirely on that of Christ. The unity and harmony in their personalities should be Christocentric, built upon "*a deep intimacy with Christ and with the Father*", in the Spirit.
>
> (*Guide for Catechists*, Congregation for the Evangelisation of Peoples, 1993, 20)

This chapter, therefore, invites you to look at your own relationship with Christ. In Chapter 2, you had the opportunity to consider if and when you had crossed the various thresholds of conversion. Maybe you discovered at that point that you did not know Jesus in a personal way. The amazing reality is that, at any point, we can begin a heart-to-heart relationship with him: "Behold, I stand at the door and knock" (*Rv* 3:20). If this is you, it may be difficult for you to complete some aspects of this chapter which presume that you are currently living as a disciple of Jesus. Don't be put off! If you feel the call to step out into this brave new world, this chapter offers a roadmap for the journey ahead.

Alternatively, maybe you know you have encountered Christ personally and have a daily relationship with him that sustains your life. You might consider yourself a disciple who has made an intentional decision to follow him.

JOURNALLING

Writing your testimony

Spend some time writing your own testimony of how knowing Jesus has changed your life.

- *Think back to a time when you did not know Jesus personally. What was your life like?*

- *What happened in your life that led you to encountering Jesus personally? Describe what happened. Recall all the details of the situation that bring it to life.*

- *What difference has this encounter made in your life? How is your life different? What do you imagine your life would be like without Jesus?*

CATECHIST TESTIMONY

"One way we can put the kerygma at the centre of our teaching is through testimony. Sometimes I think it seems easier to hide behind what we are teaching rather than share how it affects our own lives. One of my favourite learning moments came a few years ago. When teaching about Peter's denial of Jesus, I told a story from my own life. When I was about 14, some new friends asked me if I believed in God and I said no. This played on my mind all night and I was noticeably troubled. My mum wouldn't let this drop and when I eventually told her what had happened she said, 'Don't worry, even Peter denied Jesus and look what he went on to do.' The students loved this story of weakness and authentic faith. People love testimony, stories from our lives that show this isn't something we are just teaching about but something worth living and proclaiming."

Laura Thompson, RE teacher, Gumley House Convent School, Isleworth

As disciples, we are called to grow into maturity together with the whole body of Christ. At the beginning, our relationship with him might be immature and flighty; but in the end, he calls us to "maturity", to "the stature of the fullness of Christ" (see *Ep* 4:13-15). Recall *CT* 20, the goal "that the whole of a person's humanity is impregnated by [the light of God's] word". Perhaps we are a little ahead of those we catechise on the discipleship journey, but our end goal is the same.

Discipleship roadmap*

PONDER

Go back to the descriptions of a beginning disciple (see Chapter 2) and a growing disciple (see Chapter 3). Do you identify yourself in either of these descriptions?

As a growing disciple continues to grow, they realise that Jesus's mission is also their own. Sometimes, we describe this as the shift from being a *disciple* to becoming an *apostle*, one who is sent. Where a growing disciple has a heart for *God* and will make any sacrifice to grow, a commissioned disciple has a heart for *people* and will make any sacrifice to help *another* grow.

A commissioned disciple

- has decided to answer the call to take part in the mission of the Church, and
- is actively striving to win people over to Jesus and his mission, to build them up within the Church and to send them out to spiritually multiply (see *Jn* 15:8).

PONDER

Do you identify yourself in this description? Do you experience the call to make any sacrifice to help another person become a disciple?

Disciple maker

- has led someone to commit his/her life to Jesus Christ and his mission and is helping them engage in the work of evangelisation, disciple-making and friendships through a mentoring relationship (see *2 Tm* 2:2);
- has developed a heart for God's people and is willing to make any sacrifice to help another grow, even change his/her schedule (see *1 Th* 5:11); and
- makes life decisions (vocation, location, relationships, etc.) based upon how he/she can most effectively fulfil the Great Commission.

Spiritual multiplier

- has been the major influence in helping others become disciple-makers (has produced a strong third generation);
- has been trained and equipped to go to another location and remain active in lifelong Catholic mission in which this process is repeated; and
- is a regular participant in personal prayer and the sacramental life of the Church, fulfils vocational commitments, leads a life of evangelisation and discipleship through small groups; lives an influential life of faith, parish, community and workplace.

JOURNALLING

- *Reflect on each of these descriptions – beginning disciple, growing disciple, commissioned disciple, disciple maker, spiritual multiplier. Where would you place yourself on this road map?*
- *Why do you place yourself there?*
- *Where do you feel God is calling you to be on the road map? Why?*
- *What is it going to take to get there?*
- *What things do you need to do or change or sacrifice to make strides towards your goal? Are you willing to do these things?*

Growing into "the stature of the fullness of Christ" (*Ep* 4:13)

To grow in any area of our life, it helps if we *make a plan* and are *accountable to someone*.

Make a plan

- *Prayer*   Where and when will I meet with Jesus daily? How much time will I spend? How can I best have a heart-to-heart with him?
- *Scripture*   How will I fit reading Scripture into my daily plan? Will I use *lectio divina* or another way of reading the Word of God? Can I memorise short verses of Scripture?
- *Worship*   How will I praise God each day? Even when things are going badly, we grow into Christ when we intentionally praise and give thanks each day.

- *Eucharist*   Can I go to Mass more often than on Sundays? Is there an opportunity during the week when I can spend time in Adoration?

- *Reconciliation*   How frequently can I fit Confession into my schedule? How can I ensure I receive the sacrament at least monthly?

- *Silence*   How will I make time for silence in my daily life? Can I intentionally allow silence into my day to listen to God's voice?

- *Study*   How will I find time to read, listen to, or watch formation materials to increase my knowledge and understanding?

Be accountable

- *Fellowship*   Who are my friends in the faith? How can I spend more time with them? How can we make sure to share with each other what God is doing in our lives? How can we pray together?

- *Accountability*   Do you have a close spiritual friend, a priest or a fellow parishioner with whom you can regularly share your relationship with the Lord?

Growing as a disciple is not supposed to be an intense, serious journey. Every part of our lives in the world is directed towards our growth in Christ. Times of rest, relaxation and fun can be just as important as times spent in prayer. Rick Warren, the American pastor and author of bestseller *The Purpose-Driven Life*, recommends three ingredients for avoiding burnout in our lives of Christian service:

- *Divert daily*   Whatever relaxes you – a morning run, coffee with a friend, a film or good book.

- *Withdraw weekly*   God intends that one whole day of our week be used to withdraw from work and daily occupations. When we spend this day relaxing with our family and friends, we are obeying him.

- *Abandon annually*   Every year, it is healthy to disconnect completely from work, including our catechetical work. God wants to use this time each year to rejuvenate us, to remind us who we are in him, without the work that normally defines us.

Our prayer life and our catechesis

If our relationship with Christ is the most important resource for our catechesis, we have to become very sensitive to how our interior life makes an impact on this important work.

In my early days working as a parish catechetical coordinator, I learned how to get the balance right the hard way. One particularly memorable week, I contributed to a Confirmation retreat with 200 candidates on Saturday, organised the parish Confirmation Mass on Sunday, and found myself on Monday teaching a First

Communion class, a youth ministry session, and a RCIA mystagogia session. There was a lot wrong with this three-day scenario, not least that I had ridiculously unrealistic expectations for myself. I later discovered a wonderful quotation from St Bernard of Clairvaux:

> We should seek to become reservoirs rather than canals. For a canal just allows the water to flow through it, but a reservoir waits until it is filled before overflowing, then it can communicate without loss to itself. In the church today, we have many canals but few reservoirs.

It is my ongoing aim to become more of a "reservoir catechist" by planning time better, working more efficiently and blocking out time for prayer and relaxation. Some weeks I succeed better than others, but each of us is called to grow in self-knowledge about our areas of weakness:

• Do I leave things to the last minute and rush into a session with no time for prayer?

• Do I fail to block out preparation time and so find myself winging it too often in catechetical sessions?

• Is there an area of unrepented sin in my life that prevents me from being a channel of grace?

• Have I let prayer slip in my life so that I am less sensitive to the promptings of the Holy Spirit?

Chapter summary

- The mission of the catechist is a calling from God. Cooperating with the Holy Spirit, the catechist is called to make Christ known not only through their teaching, but through their whole life and manner of being.

- To be an effective cooperator with the Holy Spirit, the catechist needs a strong prayer and sacramental life, fellowship with other Christians, ongoing formation in their faith.

FATHER, I know you are calling me to more. Let me put aside the hindrances I build up, and follow you with greater confidence and zeal. Fill me with boldness to share your Son, Jesus, with those in my life. AMEN

CHAPTER 5:

Catechesis and Sacraments – How Does Catechesis Bear Fruit?

IN THIS CHAPTER...

• Consider how sacraments bear fruit in people's lives.

• Understand the role of catechesis in this fruit-bearing.

The 1986 French film *Jean de Florette* tells the story of a physically deformed tax collector, Jean, who inherits land from his mother. Two farmers, Ugolin and Papet, have been lobbying to buy the land for themselves. Jean has no intention to sell the land and has a plan to make it profitable. While the land is thought to be dry, Ugolin knows of a hidden source of water, a spring, that will solve the problem; but to thwart Jean in his plans, Ugolin blocks the spring with cement. Completely unaware of the spring, Jean struggles to irrigate his land by collecting water from another water source several miles away. It is backbreaking work, all events seem to conspire against Jean, and to add salt to the wound, he is mocked and derided by Ugolin, Papet and some of the villagers.

As I watched the film, I mused wryly that this is what catechesis often feels like. Backbreaking sowing and not much reaping. Dry, dusty land and scarce water sources. People on the side-lines wondering why we are pouring so much energy into activity that is seemingly fruitless.

Non-flowering seeds

Sometimes the Church can feel like the dry land with the blocked spring: we carry on sowing seeds because it is all we know how to do, but where is the fruit?

Many Confirmation catechists I have encountered seem to have a sad resignation that, once the beautiful Confirmation Mass is over, they will not see many of their candidates again. It is the *status quo*, and like most *status quo*s, we don't challenge it too much. Instead, we comfort ourselves with the thought that they will probably return once they want to get married or have their babies baptised. We tell ourselves, "We're just planting seeds."

We're just planting seeds. We have probably heard these words more times than we care to remember. But imagine that every autumn or spring you go into your garden and plant seeds and bulbs. When summer comes, however closely you watch, there is no sign of them germinating. Yet, faithfully, next autumn, you plant the same seeds in the same way. Summer comes. Again – no flowers.

Experience tends to form convictions in us. If we experience a reality time and again, we start to think "This is the way things are." These seeds that I am planting do not sprout or flower. It is just the way they are. Non-flowering seeds.

I wonder if, in the Church, we can become convinced that what is "normal" is no flowers, no fruit. Our only experience has been seed-sowing. "This is just the way things are." Sowing seeds, pouring resources into a black-hole vacuum, not knowing what fruit might look like, reaping a far distant reality that we have no experience of. Maybe we start to believe there is no such thing as fruit.

Perhaps the reason so many people leave the Church is because they don't see this fruit, they don't see much evidence of God alive in his Church. One 20-year-old woman who had stopped going to Mass said:

> I don't see wide signs that God is working at parish level. If Jesus Christ isn't changing hearts and transforming people then they start to get frustrated with rules and doctrine.[16]

JOURNALLING

What has been your experience in catechesis? Have you experienced being a seed-sower, a fruit-farmer or both?

My story: the blocked spring

When I was 15, like many other Catholic teenagers, I prepared for Confirmation. Let's just say that a personal relationship with God was far from being on my radar. I chose the saint's name "Monica" because she was my favourite character on the sitcom *Friends*. One of the few things I recall is being in the church as the Blessed Sacrament was exposed. I had no idea what Adoration was, and remember giggling with my friends in the front pew. Around the same time, I started going to a youth night at an evangelical church with friends from school. At these nights, I felt there was something alive in the faith of the young people around me. I knew they had something I didn't have, and if I was honest with myself, I longed for it.

What a great mystery this is. Objectively, I had received extraordinary graces in the fresh outpouring of the Holy Spirit at my Confirmation. How could it be that I seemed to be lacking something?

Thinking back to Chapter 1, and the response God invites us to make to what he has done for us, you probably have an idea of what I was lacking. *Repent – Believe – Be baptised – Be continuously filled with the Holy Spirit*. I needed to repent and believe. I needed to begin a heart-to-heart relationship with God.

God knew what he was doing. By letting me experience the faith of my evangelical friends, he was awakening a desire in me.

When I was 17, I was invited to a retreat for young people. I nearly didn't go. I only knew a few of the young people going from my parish and I was the youngest. In the end, I went. We arrived at a church hall, and the Blessed Sacrament was exposed in the centre. All around it, young people were kneeling and singing. It was abundantly clear to me that the Blessed Sacrament (whatever it was) was the centre of everything. I could see real faith in that room.

Then someone explained that this was Jesus – sacramentally present, Body, Blood, Soul and Divinity. That night, I stayed in the dim candlelight of that peaceful place, realising for the first time that this was *Jesus*, truly in front of me, truly here, the One I longed for.

The next evening, there was an opportunity to go to Confession. Before the retreat, I told my parents that if there was one thing I wouldn't do, it was to go to Confession. But, after a day of coming to terms with this incredible reality that Jesus was in the Eucharist and loved me, I couldn't say no, and that evening I found myself making the longest walk in human history: getting up from my seat and walking over to the priest. I sat down and I made a true and honest Confession, from my heart. All the sins I'd pushed to the back of my mind, I brought to him, and experienced extraordinary mercy and tenderness.

It wouldn't be an overstatement to say that that weekend turned my life upside-down. I loved Jesus in the Eucharist; I had all my sins forgiven. When I got home, my parents thought I'd gone slightly mad. I wanted to go to Mass more often; I wanted to spend time in Adoration; I started praying the Rosary.

I had gone through my childhood receiving Baptism, Eucharist, Confirmation, and all the evidence suggested that they had not changed my life. Then, all of a sudden, God broke through, and it was like a fountain of grace had exploded in my soul. It was like the spring that had been cemented over in my soul had been unblocked. My whole life was flooded with grace.

Sacraments 101

We need to understand a little more about the sacraments to dig deeper into this puzzle. Whenever any sacrament is conferred, it can be effective on three different levels.

The first level is the performing of the sacrament itself (in Latin, the *sacramentum tantum*) – the words and action (form), the matter, and the minister.

READ

In the *Catechism of the Catholic Church*, you can discover the form, matter and minister for each of the sacraments. For example, for Baptism, see *CCC* 1229 ff.

If all these elements are correct, the sacrament is validly performed and the effects are realised.

These effects are the second level of the sacrament, the *res et sacramentum*. The Latin name reveals that the effects are both reality (*res*) and sign (*sacramentum*).

They are a reality in the sense that Baptism really brings about "an indelible spiritual mark (character)" of belonging to Christ (*CCC 1272*). It is a seal that cannot be removed or repeated. You are marked for Christ forever.

It is also a sign, pointing to a reality still more ultimate. What is this fullest reality? It is the *res tantum*, the full effect of the sacrament in the life of the believer. In the case of Baptism, this is the purification of sins and new birth in the Holy Spirit (*CCC 1262*).

Imagine that a man approaches the Church, asking to be baptised, but he is living in a secret, adulterous affair. He has no intention of giving up this relationship, even though he knows it is against the law of life in Christ. He is baptised and, by virtue of the sacrament being performed correctly, the character of Baptism is conferred. He is incorporated into the Church, and his soul is sealed with an indelible spiritual mark.

But is the Sacrament of Baptism fully flourishing in his life? Has he been purified from his sins and has he experienced a new birth in the Holy Spirit? We must answer no: "Always, Baptism is seen as connected with faith" (*CCC 1226*). If a person has not responded with faith and repentance, the full effects of that sacrament will not be evident in a person's life.

If later the man realises how wrong he has been, encounters Christ, and repents of his sins, the grace of Baptism that is dormant in his soul will come alive. The spring will be unblocked.

RECAP

- You don't necessarily need to be able to explain the three levels on which a sacrament operates. But how would you explain, in simple terms, how a person can receive a sacrament validly, without its fruits being seen in a person's life? How can the full impact of the sacrament come into effect in that person's life?

- Name some ways that catechesis can best help ensure that a person receives a sacrament fruitfully.

Come alive

Sacraments like Baptism and Confirmation that confer a character on our soul are real. They have objectively changed our very being. But they can be like the hidden spring on Jean de Florette's land, not giving us the life we need. When we receive sacraments, they should come with a warning sign: "Relationship with God not included" because only in living with Christ will the sacraments explode forth with their full effect.

Pope Benedict XVI said something quite remarkable: "We are Christians only if we encounter Christ... It is only in this personal relationship with Christ, only in this encounter with the Risen One, that we are truly Christian" (September 3, 2008). It is the *encounter* that makes us come alive. If we are baptised, we are a Christian in "name" – we have God's mark on our soul. But to become a Christian in "reality" we must allow the power of Baptism to flood our lives: a real, lived, personal relationship with Christ that transforms us. Another way of putting this is to think of a gas boiler. The pilot light is always on, but when the heat comes on – pow! – there is ignition. Nicky Gumbel uses this as an analogy. He says some Christians are like "pilot light Christians" who may have been baptised, but there is no ignition. When you meet a Christian who is ignited you really notice the difference. They allow the Holy Spirit to fill their lives and are responding powerfully to what God has done for them.

Catechesis, sacraments and setting hearts ablaze

Knowing now that God wants to unleash the power of the sacraments in our lives, I hope the role of catechesis in igniting the boiler – in bringing a person to encounter God – is even more vividly clear. Catechesis is the vehicle God wants to use for starting fires in hearts.

Some years ago, I went on holiday with some friends. We stayed in a cottage in Donegal right on the edge of the Atlantic. It was miles from anywhere, the elements raged against the house, and enormous waves crashed against the cliffs. Inside the cottage we built a traditional Irish peat fire. We took it in turns to brave the elements and dig the peat turf off a pile outside the house. It took a while for this fire to get going. Sometimes the fire would catch the paper and the fire lighters but didn't engulf the heaps of turf. But once it did, once the fire enkindled these larger pieces, it made a beautiful fire whose heat spread through the whole house. It would last till the following morning.

Catechesis feeds our faith, like the big pieces of turf feed the fire. Pope John Paul II advises that catechesis should "be sufficiently complete, not stopping short at the initial proclamation of the Christian mystery such as we have in the *kerygma*" (*CT* 21). If we encounter Christ but then receive no catechesis, it is like fire catching the paper, twigs and fire lighters: for a few moments it is bright and alive, but it soon dies down and is extinguished.

But if the fire engulfs the turf, it is soon roaring and long-lasting. Similarly, if the ignited flame in our hearts is fed with catechesis, the fire of the Holy Spirit will soon engulf and take over our hearts. When this happens, our life becomes a powerful fire, giving heat and light to the whole house.

Chapter summary

- Sacraments do not bear fruit automatically; God allows us in freedom to respond to him. Only in a personal encounter with him is sacramental grace unleashed and its fruits made known in our lives.

- Catechesis allows the initial encounter with Christ to mature. It is nourishment that feeds the fire of faith, helping it grow stronger and brighter.

HOLY SPIRIT, fill me again! Fan into flames the fire within me, and burn away all that is not of you. Let the fire of your love shine through me as a powerful beacon, beckoning others into your love. AMEN.

PART 2
Content: What Do I Teach?

CHAPTER 1:

How God Longs To Redeem Us – The Four Dimensions of the Christian Life

IN THIS CHAPTER...

• Consider how the Christian life has four dimensions, displayed in the four Parts of the *Catechism*.

• Understand how the interconnectedness of the four Parts and the interweaving of the five foundational truths through the *Catechism* show the faith to be an integral whole.

• Consider a method for preparing your catechetical session.

Today it is hard to avoid in our newsfeeds and inboxes the latest health crazes: workout apps that promise to replace a gym membership; healthy-eating apps that feed us with endless new recipes; apps that measure the steps we take, how deeply we sleep, and even how many minutes of mindfulness we have achieved. Health is not measured by just one set of metrics. The health of our bodies is interconnected with the health of our minds. Each of these elements in balance is integral to the whole.

The divine pedagogy shows us that God, in accordance with how he has created us, is holistic in his way of teaching and revealing himself to us. We have seen how complex and rich the reality of evangelisation is – the many means God uses to reveal himself and lead us to him. Traditionally, the Church has categorised these ways under four headings. We call them the *four dimensions of the Christian life*. There is no app to measure whether you are firing on all cylinders for all dimensions, but you will recognise that each of these dimensions is needed in the life of a disciple.

The four dimensions are:

- *Teaching* (we need to be formed in our minds through doctrine).
- *Liturgy* (we need to be formed by allowing God to touch, transform and heal us in the sacraments).
- *Life in Christ* (we need to be formed morally through fellowship with other Christians).
- *Prayer* (we need to be formed spiritually in our interior life of prayer).

These dimensions are referred to in the life of the early Christian community: "And they held steadfastly to the apostles' teaching and fellowship, to the breaking of the bread and to the prayers" (*Ac* 2:42). If we go to Mass and Confession, but never receive teaching in the faith, pray, or share community with other Christians, it would be like exercising daily, but only ever eating doughnuts. Our health would be out of balance.

Catechesis itself, to be an "integral formation" (*GDC* 84), should include each of these four dimensions. "When catechesis omits one of these elements, the Christian faith does not attain full development" (*GDC* 87).

READ

To see what is meant by this, open a copy of the *Catechism of the Catholic Church* at the contents pages. You should see the contents table is divided into four Parts. What is the title given to each Part? What is the corresponding dimension of the Christian life (from the list above) and the corresponding word or phrase used in Acts 2:42? Completing the table below will help you see this more clearly.

Catechism of the Catholic Church	Dimension of Christian life	Acts 2:42
PART 1		
PART 2		
PART 3		
PART 4		

Throughout the Church's history, Christians have been formed according to these four dimensions, and catechisms and catechetical programmes have been structured by them. Why? Because this is how God has revealed himself to us, and how he longs to redeem us.

God's "dialogue of salvation" with us is to redeem us, to restore our inner unity and wholeness,

> until we all attain to the unity of the faith and of the knowledge of the Son of God, to mature manhood, to the measure of the stature of the fullness of Christ. (*Ep* 4:13)

CATECHIST TESTIMONY

"I have come to realise that catechesis is much more than teaching. It involves an integral formation of individuals. I have tried over the years to reflect something of what we read in Acts 2:42 in my catechetical work. My task as a catechist is to pass on to others that Deposit of Faith which has been handed down from the apostles. But the content of our faith has to become a living faith, by participating in the liturgy and sacramental life of the Church. It will also be reflected in the way I live my Christian life and in how I communicate with God in Christ and in the power of the Holy Spirit. It has been important to develop these four dimensions of Christian life in my catechesis."

Sr Veronica Brennan OP, Dominican Sisters of St Joseph

The interconnected web of mysteries

Just as the different dimensions of our physical and mental health affect each other, so are the different dimensions of faith (teaching, liturgy, fellowship, prayer) interconnected. We find that they are all interconnected in *Christ*. In catechesis, every piece of knowledge we teach (whether related to doctrine, liturgy, life in Christ, or prayer) has him at the centre. Why? Because *Christ sums up everything God has to tell us about himself.*

> In giving us his Son, his only Word (for he possesses no other), he spoke everything to us at once in this sole Word – and he has no more to say...

(St John of the Cross, quoted in *CCC* 65)

Every mystery we believe and teach in catechesis is interconnected with each of the other mysteries; and the unifying point of all these mysteries is *Jesus Christ*.

Think back to one of the first ideas we encountered about catechesis:

> The definitive aim of catechesis is to put people not only in touch but in communion, in intimacy, with Jesus Christ. (*CT* 5)

Imagine telling a friend all about this incredible man or woman with whom you had fallen in love, yet you did not want your friend to meet and get to know him or her. It wouldn't seem right. Catechesis is not just teaching knowledge *about* Jesus, it rather seeks to help someone *know him*.

Yet, to know somebody, you do need to learn more about them. Two people in love want nothing more than to talk to each other late into the night. They want to know each other. Knowledge is important because it leads to deeper love.

The *Catechism of the Catholic Church* – where all God has revealed is summarised – displays in its very structure how all the teachings of the Church are interconnected in Christ. It does this in two ways:

- Each of the four Parts is interconnected with the others, and
- The five foundational truths are woven throughout the *Catechism*.

Let's look at each of these in turn. First, *each of the four Parts is interconnected with the others*. If you turn to any page of the *Catechism*, you will see small numbers in the margin. These numbers refer to other paragraph numbers in the *Catechism*. They demonstrate how every doctrine is connected to others in an intricate web.

You will see that this is true of the entire *Catechism*. When you are using the *Catechism* to prepare catechesis, don't just stay in one Part! Use the cross-references to ensure you connect to other Parts, and therefore offer an "integral" catechesis, interconnecting the four dimensions.

The second way the *Catechism* displays the interconnection of all mysteries around Christ is that *the five foundational truths are woven throughout the Catechism*. Imagine a large, ancient oak tree. Its trunk is solid and robust, holding up the entire structure. Some branches are thicker than others; leaves and acorns adorn the tree thanks to the life received from the sturdier trunk. The tree as a whole is a beautiful sight, and would not be so without each root, twig and leaf. Yet it is the trunk that carries the other parts.

Our faith is like this:

> In Catholic doctrine there exists an order or hierarchy of truths, since they vary in their relation to the foundation of the Christian faith. (*Unitatis Redintegratio* 11)

Without the trunk, the tree could not exist; without certain foundational truths, other doctrines would not be supported.

> This hierarchy 'does not mean that some truths pertain to Faith itself less than others, but rather that some truths are based on others as of a higher priority and are illumined by them'. (*GDC* 114, quoting *General Catechetical Directory* (1971) 39)

The five foundational truths are:

- The Blessed Trinity
- The dignity of the human person
- Jesus Christ, God and man
- The Paschal Mystery
- The Church

The Catechism itself refers to how, without understanding these foundational doctrines first, it is impossible to grasp other doctrines that build on them:

- "To try to understand what sin is, one must first recognise the profound relation of man to God, for only in this relationship is the evil of sin unmasked in its true identity" (*CCC* 386).

- "The mystery of the Most Holy Trinity is the central mystery of Christian faith and life. It is the mystery of God in himself. It is therefore the source of all the other mysteries of the faith, the light that enlightens them" (*CCC* 234).

These are just two examples, but we could think of many more. For example, the teaching that Mary is Mother of God depends upon the teaching that Christ is God and man. Can you think of other examples?

RECAP

- List the four dimensions of the Christian life, and the four Parts of the *Catechism of the Catholic Church*. Why are catechisms and catechetical programmes structured in this way?
- Why is it important to understand that the teachings of the Church are interconnected in Christ?
- How does the *Catechism* display this interconnection?
- How would you explain the difference between one of the foundational truths and another of the Church's teachings?

READ

- Pierre De Cointet, Barbara Morgan and Petroc Willey, *The Catechism of the Catholic Church and the Craft of Catechesis*, Chapter 2 ("An Organic Pedagogy – Savouring the *Nexus Mysteriorum*") and Chapter 3 ("A Personal Pedagogy: Teaching the Living Realities of the Faith").
- Maryvale Institute, *Echoes: Echoing Christ – Leader's Guide* (available from CTS).

Nothing worse than last-minute Googling...

As catechists, we have all done this at some point. We realise we are teaching a session tomorrow, and don't have material ready. We start blindly Googling our topic, hoping to land upon a suitable lesson plan, a printable craft idea and, preferably, a ready-made presentation. We all know it is not the best way to approach catechesis.

In the last part of this chapter we will introduce a guide to preparing great catechesis. We will then apply this process to each of the five foundational truths in turn. You can use this process for preparing your catechesis on any topic. It is a process that allows us to dedicate time to studying the mysteries of our faith, both for our own understanding, and to consider how we would teach them to others.

As we become seasoned catechists, it is a great idea to build up our own bank of resources. This can include teachings we have prepared, stories that illustrate a point or introduce a topic well, artwork that illuminates the teaching, parts of our own testimony that fit with a particular topic. All these resources will be personal to us; we will be able more readily to teach from our own relationship with God; and it will be a lot more effective than someone else's resource dredged from the depths of the Internet!

Guide to preparing catechesis

Step 1: Prayer and *lectio divina*

Lectio divina, or sacred reading, is an ancient method for reading Scripture. It acknowledges both that Scripture is the inspired Word of God, and that the Holy Spirit indwells us as baptised Christians. It acknowledges that God speaks to us – personally and intimately – in Scripture.

Having chosen one Scripture passage related to the doctrine you are teaching:

1. Recall that you are in God's presence. Ask the Holy Spirit to fill you again.

2. Read the Scripture passage slowly.

3. Read the passage again. Is there anything you do not understand? Ask the Lord, "What does it mean?"

4. Ask yourself whether there is any situation or person from your life that this passage brings to mind?

5. Speak intimately with Jesus. Share honestly with him about anything that has come to mind.

6. Consider which word or phrase has a special meaning for you. Spend time pondering this.

7. Read the passage one more time. Close your eyes and draw close to Jesus. Listen to him. Stay in silence before God, quietly listening for him.

From your existing knowledge of this teaching, underline the key phrases from Scripture which will help you teach it.

Step 2: Read and reflect on the Proclamation

Whatever we teach, the Proclamation is the teaching in kernel form, a nutshell. If we had just ten seconds to tell someone the news, this is how we would quickly and briefly put it into words. Sometimes, catechetical resources will give you a Proclamation for a particular topic.[17] Other times, you may create one for yourself, with the help of the *Catechism*.

As we prepare and teach the session, the Proclamation should be forefront in our mind. If those we are teaching remember nothing else, we want them to remember this. When you read the Proclamation, ask yourself:

- How does this make sense of the Scripture passage I just read?
- Which part of the Proclamation do I struggle to understand?
- How is this teaching related to the kerygma? This is so important – explain this clearly and explicitly to yourself before moving on.

Step 3: Read relevant sections of the *Catechism of the Catholic Church*

- Have the Proclamation in mind throughout. This is the main message. The purpose of the catechesis is to unpack and explain the Proclamation in such a way as to deepen the understanding of those we are catechising.

- Being guided by the headings and italicised words, write down the key teaching points in your own words.[18]

- Practise explaining these points to someone in your own words.

- Practise explaining these points in relation to the kerygma.

- Ask yourself how this knowledge will lead the person you are catechising to encounter God.

Step 4: Think of your audience

When we catechise, the Church invites us to a "double fidelity". We are called to be faithful to God by handing on what we have received. We are also called to be faithful to the human person, by knowing them well. It is fatal to catechesis to become so absorbed in the content we want to teach that we forget the person we are catechising, and what they are learning and experiencing.

Think of each individual. What is going on in their lives? Do they have a living relationship with Jesus? Are they in the early stages of conversion? If the latter, we may need to put a lot of the content aside and adjust our approach (see Part 1, Chapter 2 on the thresholds of conversion). Are they in the later stages of conversion or early discipleship (check the characteristics of a beginning disciple on page 36)? If so, what questions do they have? Which areas of a topic should you particularly address? What misunderstandings might they have?

What interests, motivates, attracts them? What is their life experience and culture? What images or stories are likely to connect with them, and which will fall flat?

Step 5: Drive home the message

> The communication of the faith in catechesis is an event of grace, realised in the encounter of the word of God with the experience of the person. (*GDC* 150)

This is the step where we draw together the Word of God – the message we want to convey – with the audience to whom we are communicating. It is where the rubber hits the road. In this encounter between the Word of God and the experience of the person, the Holy Spirit is at work – he is alive in the Word, active in you, and active in the people to whom you are speaking. This is where things start to come alive! Get excited…

- How will you drive home the message?
- What images will work most powerfully? Which work of art?[19]
- How does your testimony relate to this teaching?
- Is there a story or a short video clip that will illustrate the point powerfully?
- Which point is your audience less likely to understand? How can you put more work into unpacking this point?
- How will they be invited to respond – through discussion, prayer, journalling? Which will have the greatest impact?

Step 6: Structure the session for an encounter with Christ

This is where you plan, step by step, what you will do. Use the methodology guide in Part 3 to structure your session. Think it through, step by step, putting yourself in the shoes of a person who is attending. What will be their experience, from the moment they walk through the door? At which moments will they be invited to open their hearts to God? At which point are you most likely to lose them? What conditions can be created to maximise the chance of them hearing the powerful message of God? What response are they being invited to make?

In the next chapters, we will follow this process for each of the foundational truths.

Chapter summary

- Every mystery in which we believe is interconnected and unified in Christ. This is demonstrated in the *Catechism* through the interconnectedness of the four Parts of the *Catechism*: the Profession of Faith, the Celebration of the Christian Mystery, Life in Christ and Christian Prayer.

- It is also demonstrated through the interweaving of five foundational truths, teachings of the Church that are more foundational or fundamental, and on which other doctrines depend. These are: the Blessed Trinity, the dignity of the human person, Jesus Christ, the Paschal Mystery and the Church.

- Following a guide to prepare catechesis will ensure that we prepare a session that is rooted in Scripture and the *Catechism*, that is centred on a clear Proclamation, and that unpacks the message for the particular audience we are teaching.

LORD, enlighten my mind to understand more deeply how you teach and guide us. Let my catechesis serve and be inspired by your own pedagogical action in each person's life. AMEN.

CHAPTER 2:

The Blessed Trinity

Step 1: Prayer and *lectio divina*

Choose 1 John 4:6-16 or John 14:8-11.

Step 2: Read and reflect on the Proclamation

For adults or teenagers:

God has revealed his inner secret to us: he is not alone and solitary, he is a communion of three Persons – Father, Son and Holy Spirit. The love in the heart of God is so great, he longs to share himself with us.

For younger children:

There is only one God, but in God there are three Persons. We call them by their name when we pray, "In the name of the Father, and of the Son, and of the Holy Spirit".

Step 3: Read relevant sections of the *Catechism of the Catholic Church*

> The will of God is moved by the divine beauty and goodness in an act of love

READ

Read the section on the Blessed Trinity, *CCC* 232-278.
List between three and five key teaching points.

Between three and five teaching points from the reading is optimum: more than this will be hard to communicate in just one session. Here are some examples:

• There is one God, not three Gods (see *Dt* 6:4, *CCC* 201).

• Jesus reveals that "God is one but not solitary" (*CCC* 254) and that in God there are three divine Persons (three "who") and one divine nature (one "what").

• The work of God – creation, salvation, sanctification – is the common work of the three Persons; but creation is attributed to God the Father, the first Person of the Blessed Trinity (*CCC* 238-240); redemption is attributed to the Son, the second Person (*CCC* 240-241); and sanctification is attributed to the Holy Spirit, the third Person (*CCC* 243-244).

• The inner life of God is all about love – three Persons live in a communion of perfect, self-giving love (*1 Jn* 4:6-16).

When you practise explaining these in your own words, you will soon realise whether there are parts you struggle to explain. If this is the case, put some time in to making sure you understand (the worst thing you can do is bluff it). Ask someone in your parish who has studied Theology to check whether you have understood correctly; ask your parish priest, or somebody in your diocese responsible for catechetics.

Next, explain how this teaching relates to the kerygma. For example,

> *Through Jesus, God reveals that the heart of God is love – a communion of Persons living in perfect, self-giving love. From eternity, God has wanted to share this love with every human person he created. So great was his desire to share this life of divine love with us, that God himself took on flesh, became a man, and lived among us. He did this to show us who he is. Not only that, but he wanted to remove the sin that separated us eternally from him. Jesus Christ, God in human flesh, died on the cross to remove the separation and reconcile us with the Father. When he rose on the third day, he showed that if we repent, believe and are baptised, we can be alive in him, sharing in the life of the Holy Trinity forever.*

When St Augustine set out to explain how God could be both three and one, he used several analogies based on the human person. Any analogy that is used of God is our human attempt to reach with our minds towards understanding the truth. While God has revealed himself so that we can know him *truly*, his distance from us is so vast that we cannot know him *fully*. Using analogies to increase our understanding of God is like drawing a picture of a dog and saying it has a likeness to a real, living, breathing dog. The difference between the picture and the real dog is small compared to the difference between our analogies of God and God himself.

Yet God created us with reason, and some of the greatest minds that have ever lived help us understand better the nature of God through analogy. Imagine that

God the Father looks into his divine mind and sees himself as he really is. He is all-knowing, so he knows himself perfectly. If I were to form a thought of myself, it would be imperfect because I do not know fully. My friends could tell me some things about myself that I did not know. Yet, even if I could form a perfect thought of myself, it would be only that – a thought. God's nature is different. Because it is of God's very nature to exist, it would be impossible to think of God without thinking of him as the God who always was and will be.

God's perfect thought of himself, then, must also include existence. It is his very nature to exist. The image he has of himself must have its own existence. This is a "living thought", perfectly expressing God, and we call him God the Son. God the Son perfectly expresses God's knowledge of himself: "He is the image of the invisible God" (*Col* 1:15), the "Only Begotten Son of God, born of the Father before all ages" (the Nicene Creed).

God the Father and God the Son, gazing on the divine nature they share in common, behold each other. Not only is God all-knowing; he is also all-loving. The will of God is moved by the divine beauty and goodness in an act of love. This love is infinite, living and intense. It is the love that flows eternally, the third Person "who proceeds from the Father and the Son": he is the Holy Spirit.

While we speak of the Father "begetting" the Son, and the Holy Spirit "proceeding" from the Father and Son, it is important to remember that all three are equal, infinite and eternal. It would be incorrect to think of God the Father as having "come first". Each is equally timeless.

READ

Peter J Kreeft, *Catholic Christianity* (San Francisco: Ignatius Press, 2001), Chapter 2.

Step 4: Think of your audience

When you teach the Blessed Trinity is an important question. We know that "the mystery of the Most Holy Trinity is the central mystery of Christian faith and life" (*CCC* 234), it is "the light that enlightens" all the other mysteries. In my early days as a catechist, I thought this meant that the doctrine of the Trinity should always be taught first. I remember one of the very first RCIA sessions I led, where I introduced this teaching to a group of twelve people, some of whom had barely been inside a church before. The teaching fell completely flat. However compellingly I attempted to teach it, the content was far too abstract and conceptual for people who were in the very early stages of conversion.

Many years later, I was involved in a parish where we took a different approach. One young woman had undertaken Alpha, encountered Christ and asked to be baptised. Over the next few months, through catechesis, community, and prayer, her faith deepened, and by the time she approached Baptism she was at the stage of spiritual seeking, or early discipleship. This time, we left the doctrine of the Trinity until much later. Already, she had a deep understanding of each of the three Persons – Father, Son and Holy Spirit – with whom she had a growing relationship. Following the session on the Trinity, where the difference between "nature" and "Persons" was explained, she told me how much sense it made. The catechesis had given words and terminology to a reality she already knew.

Step 5: Drive home the message

• The best illustration we can use to teach the Trinity, especially with young children, is the Sign of the Cross. To speak the words, *In the name of the Father, and of the Son, and of the Holy Spirit* is an incredible prayer. Uttering these words we give voice to our unimaginable adopted sonship in Jesus, an adoption that allows us to call God "Father".[20]

• Fra Angelico's *Baptism of Christ* can be used very effectively to teach the Trinity to adults and older teenagers. See the catechetical programme, *Anchoring You in the Faith: Anchor on the Mass*, Session 1.

• Use the traditional image below, showing the unity of the divine nature and the distinction of the Persons. This is an effective image with any age group.

• Another analogy, used by St Augustine, is to think of two people who love each other. St Augustine said, "Wherever there is love, there is a trinity: a lover, a beloved, and a fountain of love." The human family is the best example of this 'trinity': the husband and the wife love each other so much their love produces a third person, a baby.

• There are many images or analogies commonly used to teach the Trinity to children that sadly do not work. We might be tempted to think that it does not matter too much; but remember: when we speak of a mystery we are invited to do so "truly" if not "fully". Here is one example of a faulty analogy. The catechist describes how, while she is one person, she is at the same time a mother, a sister and a daughter to different people. A variation on this theme is a catechist who has three different hats – perhaps a ski hat, a sun hat and a chef's hat. Each hat represents a different activity, undertaken by the same person. What is wrong with these two analogies? Both represent a heresy concerning the doctrine of the Trinity defined as "modalism". This is the belief that God is just one Person, who reveals himself according to three different modes. But the Church has defined clearly over many centuries the reality that God is *three* Persons. While analogies like these might be attractive, we would be failing to hand on the message faithfully if we used them.

• A much better image, and one that is popular with children, is to take three long candles. You could start by having one lit as you explain that God is one. As you explain that Jesus revealed himself as God the Son, in an intimate and eternal relationship with God the Father, you could light a second candle from the first one. Finally, explain that the Holy Spirit is sent from the Father and the Son, and he is the Love that fills our hearts. Light the third candle. The three Persons are one, and to demonstrate this you can hold all three candles together to form a single flame. God is one, yet three Persons.

• For children aged 3 and up, the thirty-minute cartoon *Patrick: Brave Shepherd of the Emerald Isle* tells the story of the Saint who evangelised Ireland and used a shamrock to teach the mystery of the Holy Trinity.

• St Augustine spent decades working on *De Trinitate*, his treatise on the Blessed Trinity. A story is told that one day he was walking beside the sea, contemplating and trying to understand this great mystery about who God is. He saw a small boy running back and forth from the ocean to a small hole he had dug in the sand. He was using a seashell to carry the water and pour it into the hole. The Bishop of Hippo asked the boy what he was doing. The boy replied, "I am trying to fill this hole with the ocean." Augustine told him, "But that's impossible. That hole can't contain the whole ocean." The boy looked up and replied, "What you are trying to do is no less impossible: understand the immensity of the mystery of the Holy Trinity with your small intelligence." Augustine was amazed, and pondered what the boy had said. When he looked back, the boy had vanished. The seashell and the ocean have become a symbolic story about the limits of our minds to understand the mystery of God.

Inviting a response

• To stimulate discussion, you might ask, "Why does it matter that God is by nature a community, or a family? What difference would it make if God were *not* three Persons?"

- Take your group into the church for a time of Adoration. There is an eternal gaze of love within the heart of God among the three Persons, and it is a love from which God became man in order to draw us in. Invite the participants to spend time gazing on Christ, contemplating how he wants to draw them into the life of the Trinity.

- St Augustine famously said, "Our hearts are restless until they rest in you." Invite participants to reflect personally on how their hearts are restless. What do they long for? How are they beginning to experience rest in God? Do they see the ways that God is leading them to be fulfilled in him?

CATECHIST TESTIMONY

"We can't excuse ourselves from teaching the difficult mysteries of the Church by saying, 'It's a mystery and let's leave it as such!' A great example of this is the mystery of the Trinity. In one Catholic primary school, the children were taught to make the Sign of the Cross while saying 'From my head to my heart, from my shoulder to my shoulder, I belong to God', because it was thought to be easier for the children. In another school, I worked with a reception class who had only started school a week earlier. The children were already capable of making the Sign of the Cross and using the correct words, which their teacher had taught them. Let's not be afraid to teach these mysteries of the faith using the language of the Church."

Angela Wood, St Boniface Parish, Southampton

Step 6: Structure the session for an encounter with Christ

Use the methodology guide in Part 3 to structure your session.

GOD OUR FATHER, who by sending into the world
the Word of truth and the Spirit of sanctification
made known to the human race your wondrous mystery,
grant us, we pray, that in professing the true faith,
we may acknowledge the Trinity of eternal glory
and adore your Unity, powerful in majesty.
Through our Lord Jesus Christ, your Son,
who lives and reigns with you
in the unity of the Holy Spirit,
one God, for ever and ever.

(Collect for the Solemnity of the Most Holy Trinity)

CHAPTER 3:

The Dignity of the Human Person

> Yet you have made [man] little less than the angels… you have put all things under his feet
>
> (*Ps 8:5-6*)

Step 1: Prayer and *lectio divina*

Choose Genesis 1:26-28, Psalms 8:3-8 or 1 John 3:1-3.

Step 2: Read and reflect on the Proclamation

For adults or teenagers:

Because we are willed, loved, created and redeemed by God, we have a special dignity as his son or daughter. Every human person shares this dignity. God looks upon each person and loves them as though they were the only creature that existed.

For younger children:

God loves you so much that he made you in his image. He was thinking of you, wanting you and loving you from all eternity.

Step 3: Read relevant sections of the *Catechism of the Catholic Church*

READ

Read *CCC* 27, 355-379 in Part One, "The Profession of Faith". Cross-reference with Part Three, "Life in Christ", by reading *CCC* 1699-1709. List between three and five key teaching points.

Here are some example teaching points from the reading:

• Humans are the only creatures created for our own sake, with a desire for God and capacity to seek him (*CCC* 27).

• The reason for human dignity is that we are the only creatures called to share God's own life – this is the reason we were created (*CCC* 356). Our dignity is that of a person "who is not just something, but someone" (*CCC* 357).

• God created us spirit and matter, body and soul. Both body and soul share in the dignity of being the image of God (*CCC* 364). Together, spirit and matter in the human person form one single nature (*CCC* 365).

• God created us male and female (*Gn* 1:26-28) and both are equally in God's image. Man and woman are created together and willed each for the other (*CCC* 371).

Next, explain how this teaching relates to the kerygma. For example:

> *When we consider the dignity of what it means to be human, we are rightly amazed. We are the only creatures that bear the image and likeness of God himself. Nothing else will satisfy us but life in him. Knowing that we had damaged the image of God in us through sin, God himself came as a man to show us – not only the face of God – but the authentic face of man. This is the blessed human life he desires for us. Jesus of Nazareth willingly died upon the cross, laying down his life so that eternal life could be ours. Rising on the third day, he made possible our divine vocation. After he ascended into heaven, he sent the Holy Spirit upon the earliest disciples, so that they would become "temples of the Holy Spirit". Living in communion with each other, they even more fully displayed their likeness to God.*

Dick Hoyt's son, Rick, was born with cerebral palsy. Doctors told Dick that he would never be able to communicate or walk. But Dick would not give up on his son. Taught by his father to communicate using a computer, Rick later read an article on racing and asked to be taken running. Dick had never been a runner, but was determined to do anything for his son. He pushed Rick in his wheelchair and started to run. Rick told him that when they ran, it felt like he was not disabled. They have completed over one thousand races together including six "Ironman"s!

When we think of what people have both achieved and endured through human history, it can cause us to gasp in wonder. The Psalmist expresses this well: "Yet you have made [man] little less than the angels…you have put all things under his feet" (*Ps* 8:5-6). Yet what we are capable of physically is just a shadow of our spiritual capacity. The human person unites in himself the world of the spirit (like the angels, he has an immortal spirit) and the world of matter (he is bodily, like the animals). Body and soul are united in a person in such a close union that if I burn myself, my whole person – body and soul – feels the pain, not just my body. Similarly, if I am racked with anxiety, this will begin to show in my body. The body reveals the soul. Only in the union of body and soul together am I myself.

But it is my soul that is immortal. In the power of our intelligence and in the freedom of our will we image God in a particular way. We grow in his likeness through how we use our intelligence (knowledge) and our will (love). "For the Son of God became man so that we might become God" (St Athanasius). Our desire and capacity for God, and ultimately through transforming grace to become like him, is written into our very beings.

READ

Peter J Kreeft, *Catholic Christianity*, Chapter 4.

Step 4: Think of your audience

It goes without saying that God has been eclipsed from our culture. Not only does this mean that believing in God involves a strenuous, daily struggle against the grain of our culture, the eclipse of God also leaves the human person vulnerable to attack. When we live in a universe seemingly without God, the question "Who am I?" becomes more pressing and perplexing. What is my purpose? Why do I exist at all? Is human life "given", or can it be manipulated and controlled in any way we see fit? Does my body reveal who I am, or is it just an accessory that can be altered according to my mind? This is the air we breathe in our society, and it is the air breathed by all those whom we catechise.

Each year in our parish Confirmation programme, we would run a long session on human sexuality and relationships.[21] Outside speakers explored dating, sex and marriage. Issues such as same-sex attraction and pornography were also tackled. We soon realised we had bitten off more than we could chew. Research suggests that young people spend nine hours a day consuming media.[22] All of a sudden, in this one-and-a-half-hour session at church, they were being confronted with ideas that seemed completely foreign to them: that Catholics were not "anti-sex" but that there was a deeper and more beautiful purpose to sex than merely pleasure; that the meaning of love is far greater than warm feelings; that there is a language written into our bodies – male and female – which, if we follow it, will lead to our true fulfilment; that chastity is a virtue of strength; and that pornography fuels lust, not love, ultimately leading to our slavery and addiction.

These are ideas that are so counter-cultural, that we realised even teenagers who had been raised in Catholic families found them mind-bogglingly alien. The following year, we knew we had to dedicate much more time to the dignity of the human person. We introduced the idea of the person being someone not something (*CCC* 357) and considered practices that reduced human beings to things rather than persons. Some are obvious, for example human trafficking or abortion. Others are less obvious, for example the pressure to be very skinny or to be sexually active. Introducing these ideas earlier in the programme meant that we could continue the conversation over the many weeks that followed, before we reached the sex and relationships session.

The foundational truth of the dignity of the human person is perhaps the most important area for you really to know your audience. If they do not yet have a relationship with Christ, it is pointless to start telling someone they should not be living with their boyfriend. If someone is not yet a disciple, it makes little sense to challenge their views on homosexuality. If someone is a disciple and is therefore beginning to accept the authority of Christ and the Church, they will be more open to being challenged on the issues. But because of the prevailing norms in our culture, and how damaged people have been by lies about the human person, we must win people sensitively and gradually, acknowledging what huge lifestyle changes might be entailed for them, and what healing they might need.

One thing is for sure: the challenge to the dignity of the person is likely to become more complex, not less. Issues such as transgenderism have not been responded to definitively by the Church, and yet they are becoming more prevalent. As catechists, we need to be informed, and teach the truth always with courage, sensitivity and love.

Step 5: Drive home the message

• Session 1 of *Anchoring You in the Faith: Anchor on Confession* is a beautiful session on human dignity. It uses Georges de la Tour's *The Newborn* as a piece of art that reflects the dignity of each person.

• One way to teach children about the soul is to use a balloon demonstration. The air you blow into the balloon is invisible, but without it, the balloon is not inflated and not much use. Similarly, the soul is invisible but it gives life to the body. When a person dies, their soul leaves their body.

• Discuss with children the difference between humans, animals and plants. Having a rational soul means we can think, laugh, cry, love and decide to do what is good. Plants and animals cannot do these things. Similarly, with teenagers, ask them to name as many things as possible that show that the human person has a soul, created in God's image. As well as the ideas listed above, you could include scientific discovery, creating music, art, literature.

• Use an image of the Prodigal Son returning to his father (e.g. *Return of the Prodigal Son* by Guercino). Discuss how the son is taking off his old rags, while his father clothes him with a beautiful robe. The robe is a symbol of new life in Christ: after accepting the new life offered us in Baptism, our dignity as an adopted son or daughter of God is even greater than our natural, created dignity.

• *The Human Experience* is a great film to use with older teenagers and adults which raises lots of questions to do with human dignity. From this film, you can introduce teaching on conscience, natural moral law, the Ten Commandments and the Beatitudes.[23]

• To teach young people about living their faith in relationships, you could use the Relationships Pyramid. This is used by Pure in Heart, a movement of young adults who give presentations on the truth, beauty and meaning of human sexuality. A relationship begins with attraction (bottom of the pyramid), followed by friendship, intimacy and marriage. See Session 19 in the *Transformed in Christ* Confirmation programme for more information.

• A powerful skit which is performed to the song "Everything" by Lifehouse shows dramatically the story of a girl whose relationship with Jesus was taken over by alcohol, money and parties until she was left in a dark place. The skit shows the drama of redemption as Jesus powerfully saves her from darkness and draws her back to himself. Many examples of this skit can be found online.

• Tell children the story of Blessed Herman the Cripple. His body was terribly deformed, and he was placed in a Swiss monastery aged 7. He could barely move on his own, but he later became known as having one of the most brilliant minds of the Middle Ages. He composed the hymns *Salve Regina* and *Alma Redemptoris Mater* to Our Lady.

• Show a video clip of the Hoyts, or of Nick Vujicic, from YouTube – both demonstrate the strength of the human spirit in adversity.

• Part of the struggle of the Christian life is getting up again each time we fall. Nowhere is this truer than in the area of human dignity. A scene from *The Lord of the Rings: The Fellowship of the Ring* is a great clip to show. As Frodo finds the ring a heavy burden to bear, Gandalf counsels him that all he has to decide is what to do with the time that has been given to him. Whatever mistakes we have made in the past, we can always begin again.

• Tell teenagers or adults the story of St Maximilian Kolbe, the priest who offered his life in the place of a man who was a husband and father who had been randomly chosen by the Nazis to die. The story raises the question of freedom and what it means to be free. The idea of freedom most people have today is that it means an ability to do whatever we want. But true freedom means not to be directed by what is outside of us, in order to choose what is good. The more we do what is good, the freer we become.

Inviting a response

• To stimulate discussion, you might ask "Why does it matter that we are made in God's image? How does this make us different from other creatures?" or "Why does it matter that we are created male and female?" or "What are the biggest challenges to remembering that we are not just a body, but body and soul?"

- Use Psalm 139 or Psalm 8 as the basis for *lectio divina* with your group: this can be a powerful way to invite them to reflect on their goodness and dignity in God's eyes, and the overwhelming love of the Father for them.

- Give adults or teenagers the following two quotations to take to prayer for personal reflection:

  - *"We cannot live without love. If we do not encounter love, if we do not experience it and make it our own, and if we do not participate intimately in it, our life is meaningless."*

    (Pope St John Paul II)

  - *"The greatest proof that we are made in the image and likeness of God is that only love makes us happy, only love fulfils us."* (Pope Benedict XVI)

Step 6: Structure the session for an encounter with Christ

Use the methodology guide in Part 3 to structure your session.

O GOD, who restore human nature
to yet greater dignity than at its beginnings,
look upon this amazing mystery
of your loving kindness,
and in those you have chosen to make new
through the wonder of rebirth
may you preserve the gifts
of your enduring grace and blessing.
Through our Lord Jesus Christ, your Son,
who lives and reigns with you
in the unity of the Holy Spirit,
one God, for ever and ever.

(Collect for the Mass of Thursday of the Fourth Week of Easter)

CHAPTER 4:

Jesus Christ: True God and True Man

Step 1: Prayer and *lectio divina*
Choose Colossians 1:15-20 or John 1:1-18.

Step 2: Read and reflect on the Proclamation
For adults or teenagers:
In the fullness of time, God sent his only-begotten Son, Jesus Christ, to save us. In him, God showed us how much he loved us by becoming one of us, by experiencing everything we experience except sin.

For younger children:
God the Father sent Jesus as the light of the world. Jesus is God, the Second Person of the Holy Trinity, but he was born into the world as a child like us.

Step 3: Read relevant sections of the *Catechism of the Catholic Church*

> The poor people all over the earth who have never heard of Jesus, they are the poorest people

READ

Read CCC 422-424, 430-478 in Part One, "The Profession of Faith". List between three and five key teaching points.

Here are some example teaching points from the reading:

• From the earliest moment after the Original Sin, God the Father planned to save his people (see *Gn* 3:15), preparing his people for a Saviour (*CCC* 422). The plan is brought to fulfilment when the Holy Spirit overshadows Mary and God the Son takes on flesh in her womb – Jesus (*Lk* 1:26-38).

• The Son of God became man for four principal reasons: to reconcile us to God by dying for our sins (*CCC* 457); so that we might know God's love (*CCC* 458); to be our model of holiness (*CCC* 459); to make us partakers in the divine nature (*CCC* 460).

• Jesus is one divine Person with two natures – divine and human. He is fully God and fully man (*CCC* 464).

Explain how this teaching relates to the kerygma. For example:

> *Seeing how his people were enslaved in a cycle of sin, unable to save themselves, God did the unimaginable. He himself took on human flesh and became man – Jesus. Though fully God, Jesus lived a fully human life and experienced everything we experience. He knows our joys, our sufferings and our pain. To show the extent of his love, and to reconcile us to the Father, he died a humiliating and painful death on a Cross, saving us forever from sin and death. As he died, he had in mind every single human being who would ever live. He knew the sins we would commit for which he would die. And he loved us and chose to die for us anyway. Whenever we feel trapped in a cycle of sin, we can cry out to Jesus, our Saviour.*

Sometimes we might have a tendency in catechesis to emphasise the humanity of Jesus above his divinity. We want people to know how fully Jesus knows the human condition; and, of course, this is vital. But what is remarkable in the New Testament is how Jesus claims something scandalous and incomprehensible – he identifies himself with God. In John 8:51-59 he provokes a reaction so strong that people pick up stones to throw at him. In Luke 5:20-26 and in other passages, he is accused of speaking blasphemies. This is not a tame, domesticated Jesus who would never offend anyone. This is not merely a wise moral teacher or guru who teaches us to "be kind". What he is claiming is unmistakable, and it is earth-shattering.

In John 8:58, Jesus astonishes his hearers when he declares, "Before Abraham was, I am." Knowing a little of the Old Testament, we recall that in Exodus 3:14, God revealed his Name to Moses in the burning bush, "I am who I am." If what he is claiming is not true, it is clearly blasphemous. In Mark 14:62 Jesus, on trial before the Sanhedrin, reveals he is "the Christ, the Son of the Blessed", alluding back to Deuteronomy 7:13-14, where the Son of Man is depicted, the Messiah who will save Israel. In Luke 5:24, he claims that "the Son of man has authority on earth to forgive sins" – something only God can do – when he commands the paralysed man to stand and walk. Jesus's claims are scandalous and we should avoid domesticating him in our catechesis. After all, only One who is God can save us from our sins; we need a Saviour who is fully human and fully divine.

READ

Peter J Kreeft, *Catholic Christianity* (San Francisco: Ignatius Press), Chapter 5.

Step 4: Think of your audience

Whenever we proclaim Jesus, we know we are standing in the most sacred and privileged moment of our vocation as catechists. We are here to tell people about *Jesus*. The One who saves. The answer to the hunger of every human heart. His is "the one name that contains everything…that the Son of God received in his incarnation: JESUS… To pray 'Jesus' is to invoke him and to call him within us. His name is the only one that contains the presence it signifies" (*CCC* 2666). When we speak about Jesus in our catechesis, we are not sharing interesting ideas or concepts – we are proclaiming him who, if we draw close to him, will not leave us unchanged.

In the 1960s, aged 22, Jackie Pullinger boarded a ship with a one-way ticket and disembarked in Hong Kong. She ended up in a place called The Walled City, a slum district which fell under the jurisdiction neither of Hong Kong nor of China, and so was a place of gangs, drugs and prostitution. In this place of darkness, Jackie felt called to tell people about Jesus. She thought to herself, "Now, if Jesus walked down this street, what would He do? And I knew nobody would be the same after He walked past." She has since worked for decades with drug addicts in this district, many of them giving their lives to Christ. She says, "The poor people all over the earth who have never heard of Jesus, they are the poorest people."

What are the needs of the people you are catechising? What are their fears, addictions or shame? Where do they need a Saviour? Pray before you teach about Jesus. Ask him to touch and change the lives of those you catechise. Know that even speaking his Name evokes his Presence. Come, Lord Jesus, do not delay.

Step 5: Drive home the message

• With an RCIA group, you might decide to start with one of the Gospels (e.g. St Luke) and read a little together each week and discuss people's reactions to it. It is powerful to simply read the Gospel unmediated and allow the Person of Jesus, Word of God, to be revealed.

• William Holman Hunt's *Light of the World* is a striking image to use when teaching about Jesus. Jesus comes in the night, symbolising the darkness of the world, carrying a lantern, symbolising his grace. The garden is overgrown and weeds grow over the door. These symbolise the sin and ignorance of the soul without Christ. Christ is knocking on the door, and you will notice there is no handle on the outside of the door. When asked about this, Hunt replied, "It is the door of the human heart, and that can only be opened from the inside."

• Hearing the miracles and parables of Jesus in the Gospels is a direct way of hearing who he is. A wonderful catechetical programme for children aged 7 to 11 which achieves this effectively is *Come, Follow Me*.[24] The aim of the programme is to lead children increasingly into a relationship with God.

• With teenagers, take passages from the Gospels and invite them to match them to the Old Testament prophecies they fulfil. This demonstrates how the Old Testament is fulfilled by the New, and how the New Testament is hidden in the Old. See Session 7 in the *Transformed in Christ* Confirmation programme for an example.

• If you have already taught the terms "Person" and "nature" while teaching the Blessed Trinity, you can re-introduce them here. "Nature" means "what you are" while "person" means "who you are." Jesus has two natures – he is both God and man. The union of these two natures in one Person is a mystery of our faith. The result of this union is one Person always acting in harmony, as one identity.

• To consolidate how Jesus is both fully God and fully man, read statements such as "Jesus was conceived by the Holy Spirit" or "Jesus was the son of Mary" and invite participants to say whether this reveals he is fully God or fully man. To make it more fun, give participants two-sided signs – one side reading "fully God" and the other, "fully man". At each statement, they hold up the correct side of the sign.

• Share stories of how Jesus has transformed people's lives – most powerful are the testimonies from people in your own parish.

• The *Catholicism* film series produced by Word on Fire starts with two very attractive and compelling films on Jesus – *Amazed and Afraid: The Revelation of God Become Man* and *Happy Are We: The Teachings of Jesus*.

• Use clips from *Jesus of Nazareth* or *The Bible: The Epic Mini-Series* as an introduction or illustration of your teachings on Jesus.

Inviting a response

• To stimulate discussion, you might ask, "Some people claim Jesus was no more than a good moral teacher. How would you respond to this?" or "What evidence is there that people need a Saviour?" Ask people to reflect personally on the question of where they need a Saviour in their own lives. If we don't know our need of salvation, we cannot know the full power of Jesus in our lives.

• Use Mark 10:46-52, the story of Jesus healing a blind man, for *lectio divina* or a guided meditation. Jesus asks the question "What do you want me to do for you?" (*Mk* 10:51) Invite the participants to spend time intimately with Jesus in prayer – how do they respond to Jesus's question?

- Use the opportunity of speaking about Jesus to invite people to make a personal response. Remember the response that we are continually invited to make: Repent, Believe, Be Baptised, Be Continuously Filled with the Holy Spirit. Invite people to make an act of faith in Jesus, perhaps for the first time, using the prayer on page 36. Or you can invite people to renew their faith in Jesus, by renewing their baptismal promises.

Step 6: Structure the session for an encounter with Christ

Use the methodology guide in Part 3 to structure your session.

O GOD, Creator and Redeemer of human nature,
who willed that your Word should take flesh
in an ever-virgin womb,
look with favour on our prayers,
that your Only Begotten Son,
having taken to himself our humanity,
may be pleased to grant us a share in his divinity.
Who lives and reigns with you
in the unity of the Holy Spirit,
one God, for ever and ever.

(Collect for the Mass of Weekdays of Advent, December 17)

CHAPTER 5:

The Paschal Mystery

Step 1: Prayer and *lectio divina*

Choose Philippians 2:5-11, Mark 10:32-45 or Matthew 26:17-30.

Step 2: Read and reflect on the Proclamation

For adults or teenagers:

Jesus Christ, God in the flesh, willingly died for us to save us forever. He wanted to give us his eternal life, and in exchange, would suffer our death, despair and abandonment, so as to share with us in everything.

For younger children:

When Jesus died on the Cross, he showed how great the Father's love is for you, and how much he wanted you to live with him in Heaven forever.

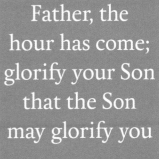

Father, the hour has come; glorify your Son that the Son may glorify you

(*Jn* 17:1)

Step 3: Read relevant sections of the *Catechism of the Catholic Church*

READ

Read *CCC* 517, 595-667 in Part One, "The Profession of Faith" and *CCC* 1077-1090 in Part Two, "The Celebration of the Christian Mystery". List between three and five key teaching points.

Here are some example teaching points from the reading:

- Jesus, in loving obedience to the Father, bore our sins and offered his life for our salvation. His Death was according to the plan of the Father (*CCC* 599), who showed how his plan is one of benevolent love for us by giving up his own Son (*CCC* 604). Jesus was united to the Father's will by loving us to the end (*CCC* 609).

- Christ's death is the Paschal sacrifice that definitively redeems us (*CCC* 613). Though it is a unique sacrifice for all time, he invites us to participate in it and make it our own (*CCC* 618). We participate in the Paschal Mystery in the sacraments.

- Jesus Christ showed that he defeated death forever and fulfilled all that he promised when he rose on the third day. Many were witnesses to his Resurrection and his new, glorious body (*CCC* 642).

- God's plan entered its fulfilment when Christ ascended into Heaven (*CCC* 670). This showed definitively that humanity has now entered heaven through Christ, that Christ is Lord, that all things are subject to him (*CCC* 668).

The teaching of the Paschal Mystery is perhaps closest among all the teachings of our faith to the message of the kerygma itself.

RECAP

In your own words, how would you summarise the Paschal Mystery?

Sometimes people may not have heard the Passion, Death, Resurrection and Ascension of Jesus referred to as the "Paschal Mystery". The word Paschal refers to the Passover, the Jewish feast that was celebrated at the time of Jesus's death. We understand from the timings of the events of the Passion that Jesus is the Paschal Lamb - he is the blood ransom, saving us from death.[25] "Paschal Mystery" is often short-hand for referring to these events.

When we teach the Paschal Mystery, we are standing on the threshold between two Parts of the Catechism - "The Profession of Faith" and "The Celebration of the Christian Mystery" – and it is vital that we make this connection come alive. What is unique about Jesus's Paschal Mystery is that it is not merely a past event that we remember because it brought our salvation. That would be amazing enough. But there is more. The liturgy – and in a pre-eminent way the Mass – doesn't just commemorate the mystery of Jesus's Passion, Death and Resurrection, *it makes it present, right here, right now*. I remember the first time I realised this when I was 17 years old, and I never saw Mass the same again. It dawned on me that Mass was being offered in my parish church every single day, and that Jesus's sacrifice on the Cross on Calvary was being made present, right there. It awoke in me a desire to go to Mass as often as I could.

Occasionally people ask why God would send his Son to die. It makes God the Father seem cruel and deep down we wonder if we can trust him if this is what he allowed to happen to his Son. But this would be to view the Persons in God too humanly, as beings with separate wills. We know that, as a Divine Person, Jesus had one will, united with the Father's. His human soul and body suffered immensely, knowing the agony that awaited him. But he shared completely his Father's love for humanity and, "embracing in his human heart the Father's love for men, Jesus 'loved them to the end' (*Jn* 13:1)" (*CCC* 609). The Father and Son were inseparable in their mission to save us. John's Gospel in fact reveals the Cross as Christ's glory; his prayer to the Father makes this clear: "Father, the hour has come; glorify your Son that the Son may glorify you" (*Jn* 17:1). He willingly and lovingly chose the sacrifice, and the Gospels attest to many ways in which Jesus appears to be in control of the circumstances of his Passion. While it appeared on the surface humiliating weakness and defeat, everything that occurred fulfilled God's plan. As St Peter put it, "this Jesus [was] delivered up according to the definite plan and foreknowledge of God" (*Ac* 2:23).

Nowhere is it clearer that the victory belongs to God than at the Resurrection when Jesus's glory is no longer hidden but manifested – he is alive! All his promises have been true: "When you have lifted up the Son of man, then you will know that I am he" (*Jn* 8:28).

READ

Peter J Kreeft, *Catholic Christianity* (San Francisco: Ignatius Press), Chapter 5.

Step 4: Think of your audience

Ask yourself where the stumbling blocks might be for your audience. Firstly, do they have a sense of sin in their life, an awareness that they need saving? Sometimes this can come quite late in the conversion towards discipleship. In our culture, it is uncommon to have a sense of personal sin. To begin to awaken this awareness, it is helpful to share your own experience. Give examples of when we might experience guilt. Some things that make us feel guilty might not be sin (for example, the outcome of a situation you could do nothing to change) but other times, we know that we should have done something differently. We know we have damaged our relationship with God and others. As well as sin, Jesus wants to save us from all despair, suffering and abandonment in our life. Jesus's death conquers forever anything that separates us from God.

Secondly, how can you help them to grasp that an event that happened 2000 years ago saved them from their sins? Knowing that God has become man and walked on earth changes everything about history. The pivotal moment of all time is Jesus's life, death and resurrection. This is the lens through which we now see everything else –

every event in history, every human person that has ever lived: "There is not, never has been, and never will be a single human being for whom Christ did not suffer" (Council of Quiercy, *CCC* 605).

Pope John Paul II wrote something profoundly inspiring to the catechist:

"The man who wishes to understand himself thoroughly – and not just in accordance with immediate, partial, often superficial, and even illusory standards and measures of his being – he must with his unrest, uncertainty and even his weakness and sinfulness, with his life and death, draw near to Christ. He must, so to speak, enter into him with all his own self, he must "appropriate" and assimilate the whole of the reality of the Incarnation and Redemption in order to find himself. If this profound process takes place within him, he then bears fruit not only of adoration of God but also of deep wonder at himself" (*Redemptor Hominis* 10).

This process of "appropriating" the reality of the Incarnation and Redemption – of understanding our human experience through this lens – is vital for the catechist. Only then will we be able to speak personally and convincingly of the Paschal Mystery.

Step 5: Drive home the message

• In St Catherine of Siena's *Dialogue* she shares an image given her by God the Father of a wide, stormy river, representing sin, that separated humanity from God. People are drowning in the river because it is impossible to cross with only human effort. God the Father tells St Catherine how he gave a bridge – his Son – so that we may cross the river without being drowned. This bridge is vast and stretches between Heaven and Earth. The bridge analogy can be a very helpful way to teach Redemption. The Catholic Christian Outreach faith study series, *Discovery*, offers a helpful outline for teaching how Christ saves us based on this analogy.[26]

• The mosaic in the apse of the Basilica di San Clemente in Rome is a striking image for teaching about salvation. The Crucifixion is unusual because the scene seems to be teeming with life. At the foot of the Cross, two deer are drinking from a stream. Luscious green foliage is sprouting from the Cross and filling the apse. A clear connection is being drawn between the Crucifixion and the tree of life. Jesus's Death is the source of our life.

• It is a difficult mental leap to imagine that Jesus died for the sin of the whole world. We can make it more concrete by inviting participants to imagine all the sins they have ever committed in one heap. Imagine all of this was carried on the back of another person. Now imagine all the sins of people in the room heaped upon that person too. Next add all the sins of everyone in your parish, then everyone in your town. This is an enormous amount of sin. Jesus bore the burden of sin not just of one town, but of the whole world. This includes all those who existed in the past, and all those who will be born in the future. He was God so he could bear it, but he was also human so his suffering was immense.

- To show how the Paschal Mystery is made present in the Mass, invite participants to read Eucharistic Prayer I together. Find references to Jesus's sacrifice. When the Mass is offered, who is offering the sacrifice? To whom is it being offered?

- As a group, pray together the Way of the Cross around your church. Or pray the Sorrowful or Glorious Mysteries of the Rosary.

- Use the clip from the Passion in *The Bible: The Epic Mini-Series* (rated 12) as an introduction or illustration of your teachings on Jesus.

- For young children, show the cartoon with Brother Francis, *He is Risen*, on the resurrection.

- Tell your group about the Shroud of Turin, believed to be the burial cloth of Jesus. A very detailed image on the cloth is believed to be an imprint of the face of Jesus. The marks of the nails in Our Lord's hands and feet can be seen, the wounds from the scourging and crown of thorns, and the wound in his side from the soldier's spear.

- The short film clip, *Falling Plates*, is a powerful summary of the kerygma (see www.fallingplates.com).

Inviting a response

- To stimulate discussion, you might ask "Why did Jesus need to die? Why couldn't God have forgiven our sins another way?" or "Why is it important to believe in Jesus's bodily Resurrection?"

- Peter Kreeft, a Catholic philosopher, asks many of his students the following question: "If you were to die tonight and God were to ask 'Why should I let you into heaven?', what would you say?" Often people will list what they do to show their response to God. But the real answer to this question can only be *Jesus*. It is only thanks to his Death and Resurrection that I have freely received forgiveness and can be saved.

- While Jesus has laid down his life as a bridge for us to return to God the Father, our salvation does not end there. We have to get onto the bridge and walk across it. We have to respond with *Repentance – Belief – Baptism – Being Continuously Filled with the Holy Spirit*. Invite those who would like to make a response to Christ to come forward. Invite them to pray an act of faith like the one on page 36. You could also pray for those who would like to give their lives more wholeheartedly to Christ.

CATECHIST TESTIMONY

"One of the hardest things for many catechumens to understand is the Church's take on suffering and evil in the world. How can a good God let suffering exist? In looking at the Paschal Mystery – the passion, death, resurrection, and ascension of Christ – we find the answer, though maybe not the one we expect, or would like. The Church is in the business of proclaiming the truth, and so she would never make us impossible promises of a life without suffering, but she can offer consolation and purpose. Christ's life and death have transformed suffering. There is nothing beyond His saving power: even death can be made to serve good ends when combined with love. This is such a hard teaching, but as suffering is universal, it's one we need to address in RCIA and sacramental preparation. When we suffer it can challenge our faith and make us feel worthless and unloved by God, but in the Paschal Mystery we see a pattern to overcome such despair. The cross is gruesome, scandalous, and disgusting to see, but its horror nonetheless radiates more love and life than we can find anywhere else. One challenge of a Christian life is to incorporate this paradox into our own approach to suffering, and to be willing to suffer with Christ in order to become like Him."

Victoria Seed, Holy Trinity and St Augustine of Canterbury Catholic Church, Baldock

Step 6: Structure the session for an encounter with Christ

Use the methodology guide in Part 3 to structure your session.

O GOD, who restore us to eternal life
in the Resurrection of Christ,
raise us up, we pray, to the author of our salvation,
who is seated at your right hand,
so that when our Saviour comes again in majesty,
those you have given new birth in Baptism
may be clothed with blessed immortality.
Through our Lord Jesus Christ, your Son,
who lives and reigns with you
in the unity of the Holy Spirit,
one God, for ever and ever.

(Collect for the Mass of Friday of the Sixth Week of Easter)

CHAPTER 6:

The Church

The Church has four characteristics: she is one, holy, catholic and apostolic

(CCC 811-870)

Step 1: Prayer and *lectio divina*

Choose Acts 2:41-47 or Matthew 16:13-19.

Step 2: Read and reflect on the Proclamation

For adults or teenagers:

From the beginning, God has desired all people to be in communion with him and with each other, in the Church. The Church is God's mission to bring salvation to the ends of the earth.

For younger children:

The Church is the family of all baptised people. The Church brings the Good News about Jesus to everyone.

Step 3: Read relevant sections of the *Catechism of the Catholic Church*

READ

Read *CCC* 748-870 in Part One, "The Profession of Faith". List between three and five key teaching points.

Here are some example teaching points from the reading:

• God the Father has intended the Church from the beginning as the place where salvation is accomplished (*CCC* 759-760); the Church was instituted by Jesus Christ (763-766) and is filled with the Holy Spirit as the soul fills the body (*CCC* 767-768).

• Certain titles for the Church help us understand more about her character: People of God, Body of Christ, Temple of the Holy Spirit (*CCC* 781-801).

• The Church has four characteristics: she is one, holy, catholic and apostolic (*CCC* 811-870).

Explain how this teaching relates to the kerygma. For example:

> *God made human beings in his image. He intended them to love and be loved. God himself is not a solitary being and he does not call us to heaven by ourselves. Jesus died for each of us individually on the cross, but he wanted us to be saved together. In the Church's earliest form, Jesus gathered twelve disciples, and built them up around Peter, the rock (Mt 16:18). When he ascended into heaven, Jesus instructed the disciples to go, make disciples, baptise and teach (Mt 28:19-20) and this is still the reason the Church exists today.*

When I was 17 and encountered Christ for the first time, it was also my first experience of the Church fully alive. Young people who gathered to sing and pray together were on fire at having met Jesus and their passion was infectious. In the times of fellowship during the retreat, I felt a deep bond with brothers and sisters with whom I would never normally be friends. We had discovered something amazing together – not only a relationship with Christ, but an experience of community we had not imagined possible.

We are made for communion. Communion with others in the Church originates from our communion with Christ. This is why the bonds between Christians who have encountered Christ are bonds deeper than those forged by any other human activity. Why? Because we have divine life in us, the sanctifying grace of the sacraments. Even now, in communion with other Disciples of Christ, we have a foretaste of the divine life and communion of the Blessed Trinity.

We need community, and we also need visible assurance of what we know to be true. The Church is not just a spiritual reality. Just as he took on flesh as a human, Christ established the Church as something visible – a living voice that continues to proclaim Christ's teachings through the centuries (magisterium) and visible channels through which we can receive healing and grace (sacraments).

READ

Peter J Kreeft, *Catholic Christianity*, Chapter 7.

Step 4: Think of your audience

The Church is sometimes called the "sacrament of salvation" (*CCC* 774-776). An encounter with the Church should be an encounter with Christ. Sometimes we experience this in a wonderful way. Think back to the stories of Tom, Rachel, Mark and Angela in Chapters 2 and 3. Each of them, as part of their journey towards discipleship, experienced community that was compelling, drawing them deeper into a relationship with Christ. But often our experience of the Church does not meet that longing for deep, intimate friendship with others in Christ. At times, it can be hard to find others with whom to discuss our relationship with God.

When we present teaching on the Church, we will inevitably teach essential facts: the four marks of the Church; that the Church is divine and human. But how do these teachings relate to the participants' experience of the Church? If we speak passionately about the Church as Body of Christ, but their experience of the parish is that no one speaks to them, there is a disconnection. What we profess to believe is not being lived out. It is here that we see how the four dimensions of the Christian life are interrelated. Teaching on the Church and experience of the Church should tell the same story. Otherwise, to those becoming or growing as disciples, it is not very convincing.

Step 5: Drive home the message

• The Church is the Deposit of Grace, and the seven sacraments are the main channels by which we receive this grace. Use van der Weyden's *Seven Sacraments Altarpiece* as an image to introduce the sacraments.

• The cathedral of Our Lady of the Angels in Los Angeles has enormous tapestries down both sides of the nave, depicting saints throughout the centuries. They are stylised as contemporary figures. Among the 135 saints and blesseds are twelve anonymous figures, suggesting that we too are called to be numbered among the saints. Images of these tapestry frescoes can be found online.

• The *Catechism* uses many images to teach about the Church: the People of God, the Body of Christ, a sheepfold, a family, a temple (see *CCC* 754-757). Use these images to teach what is revealed about the nature of the Church.

• There are many different works of sacred art that depict the Church in her three states: on earth, suffering in purgatory, triumphant in heaven. One example is Quarton's *The Coronation of the Virgin*.

• To show that the Church was in the Father's plan from the beginning, we can use the timeline of salvation history. Five Old Testament covenants were embodied in different groupings of people: a couple, a family, a tribe, a nation and a kingdom.

Finally, in the Church, God wants his salvation to reach the whole world: anyone who believes in Christ can be baptised and become a member of the Church.

• Praying the Liturgy of the Hours is a way of being united with the universal Church throughout the world.

• Share testimonies of people who have become Catholic, often at great personal cost. A film that shares many such stories is *Convinced* (available on https://formed.org).

• Whether with children or adults, sharing stories of saints throughout your programme (not just when you teach about the Church) is a way of illustrating the breadth and depth of the Church. There are countless different personalities and ways of holiness.

Inviting a response

To stimulate discussion, you might ask "Why do we need the Church? Can't people simply have a relationship with God without going to church?" or "Why is the Church hierarchical and not democratic?"

Lead participants in a meditation. If being a disciple of Christ means being responsible for the Church's mission, do they feel ready to accept this mission? What is holding them back from making the mission of the Church their own?

Step 6: Structure the session for an encounter with Christ

Use the methodology guide in Part 3 to structure your session.

O GOD, who from living and chosen stones
prepare an eternal dwelling for your majesty,
increase in your Church the spirit
of grace you have bestowed,
so that by new growth your faithful people
may build up the heavenly Jerusalem.
Through our Lord Jesus Christ, your Son,
who lives and reigns with you
in the unity of the Holy Spirit,
one God, for ever and ever.

(Collect for the Mass of the Feast of the Dedication of the Lateran Basilica)

PART 3
Methodology: How do I teach?

CHAPTER 1:

Why Does It Matter How a Session is Structured?

IN THIS CHAPTER...

• Consider how the method we use for catechesis should be inspired by the pedagogy of God.

• Understand how method is at the service of revelation and conversion, and what the practical implications of this are.

Education today, at whatever level you teach, can be a minefield. New teachers find themselves drowning in assessment criteria, classroom observations and impossible piles of marking. Within the field, there is endless debate about how students best learn: how interactive should they be? How much talking should the teacher do? Could students in fact teach themselves given the best learning environments? Educational psychologists identify different types of learning tendency: certain students will learn best through small group discussion and projects, while others will need opportunities to think alone.[27]

While some understanding of educational theory can be helpful to a catechist, the good news is that catechesis is *not* like education in any other field. In fact, it is completely unique.

Maybe your parish priest asked you to become a catechist because you are a teacher by profession. Skills you learn as a teacher will undoubtedly help you as a catechist. However, beware. Some of the methodological approaches you are familiar with may not.

Why?

READ

Read again the section in Part 1, Chapter 3 on the pedagogy of God.

Method inspired by God's pedagogy

By pedagogy of God, we understand that God himself teaches, and that as catechists, we serve God's own pedagogy in the lives of those who are catechised. One practical way we can highlight that God himself is the one who teaches is to take recourse to him frequently through the session: "Let's pause and ask the Holy Spirit to shed light on our understanding..."; "If God has prompted our conscience in some way, let us take this to him in prayer at the end..."; "Let us be aware that God wants to do wonderful things for us during this process... [e.g. RCIA]"; "Let us thank him for the insights and grace we have received..."

PONDER

How could you do this in your next catechetical session?

Even more than this, the Church teaches that our catechesis should not only *serve* but *be inspired by* God's own pedagogy. In other words, how God teaches should inform how we teach.

Let's look at what the Church teaches on this in the *General Directory for Catechesis*:
- "The Church, in transmitting the faith, does not have a particular method nor any single method. Rather, she discerns contemporary methods in the light of the pedagogy of God" (*GDC* 148).
- "The catechist recognises that method is at the service of revelation and conversion" (*GDC* 149).
- "A good catechetical method is a guarantee of fidelity to content" (*GDC* 149).

Whether a certain methodology is suitable for catechesis is always assessed in the light of the divine pedagogy. Does it make God's revelation known in its truth or does it obscure it? Does it help a person towards conversion? Does the method support or undermine the truth of the content?

PONDER

In the following examples, decide whether the methodology used is suitable or not for catechesis. Use the questions above to help you assess each case. (You will find comments on each of the examples at the end of this chapter.)

Example 1

Rachel's youngest child has started going to Children's Liturgy of the Word by herself. The group processes out of the church with a children's Book of the Gospels, and into the church hall. A corner of the room is laid out beautifully with a reverently displayed Bible, a candle, and an icon or work of sacred art according to the Gospel of the week. Quiet music is playing and the environment feels sacred and quiet. The children begin with an age-appropriate Penitential Act, followed by the reading of the Gospel for which they stand, sing the Gospel Acclamation and sign a cross on their forehead, lips and heart. After the Gospel, they sit down, and the catechist proclaims a simple message from the Gospel they have heard, before unpacking this message with examples, discussion and varied illustrations. Prayers of intercession follow. When these have finished, they have a short time of quiet prayer before they go back into the church at the time of the Offertory.

Example 2

Mark's middle son, Pete, has reluctantly agreed to sign up for Confirmation classes. After his own conversion, Mark has never been keener that his children come to know the Lord in the way he has over the last year. Pete does not regularly come to Mass, but Mark is hoping that his experience at Confirmation classes will change that. At the first session, Pete arrives nervously, not knowing any of the other young people on the course. The church hall seems to be in chaos as he enters, and after his name is ticked off a list, he looks around to see different groups of young people gathered in different corners, with no apparent organisation. He recognises one of his old friends from primary school and they end up hanging around with a group of boys until finally someone calls them to sit down. A catechist organises a game for which she forgets the instructions, and so abandons it halfway through. A retired priest based in the parish comes to speak to them, but after fifteen minutes of monotonous memories about his own Confirmation, most of the young people have switched off. The ropey start has succeeded in uniting Pete and the group of boys he met: they giggle through each of the activities and by the time the catechist has stood up to give the next instructions, one of them starts heckling. Splitting into small groups, Pete and his new group of friends begin to think that, although they thought Confirmation would be boring, they might as well make the most of it and have some fun, even if it is at the expense of these underprepared catechists.

Integral formation

Before thinking further about how the method we use can either serve or hinder God's revelation, let us consider some more factors we can learn from God's pedagogy:

• God teaches us by means of an **integral formation** (see *GDC* 84) according to the four dimensions of the Christian life (see the beginning of Part 2 above). Throughout salvation history, God revealed himself not just through words and teaching, but through signs and deeds, liturgy and prayer, and the making of covenants whereby he forms his People progressively into a nation through whom the entire world will know salvation. The *GDC* speaks of this as "a pedagogy of signs, where words and deeds, teaching and experience are interlinked" (*GDC* 143).

• God teaches **progressively**. Over thousands of years of Old Testament history, "God communicates himself to man gradually. He prepares him to welcome by stages the supernatural Revelation that is to culminate in the person and mission of the incarnate Word, Jesus Christ" (*CCC* 53). In our own lives, too, God teaches us progressively, not revealing everything about himself at once.

• God teaches people both through proclaiming the message, on which people reflect, applying it to their lives, and through allowing people to reflect on their own problems and conditions, before enlightening these with the Word of God. The first approach is known as the **deductive method**, and the second as the **inductive method** (*GDC* 150-151). Both methods can be used in catechesis. The deductive method starts with the message itself; the second starts with experience, enlightening it with the word.

• God respects the dignity and freedom of the human person. St Bernadette spoke to this when she said, "I was not instructed to convince you, but to tell you." It is not our job to persuade, but to announce. At the end of the Annunciation account there is the striking line: "And the angel left her." Mary is free to respond, and in the same way, as catechists, we are asked only to invite and propose. If we limit the freedom of a person in any way, we are hindering God's pedagogy.

Let us consider some more examples. For each one, think about how it serves or hinders the pedagogy of God, referencing the factors above.

Example 3
In the first session of RCIA, which lasts an hour and a half, the group explore the desire of the human person for God, the proofs for the existence of God and the doctrine of the Blessed Trinity.

Example 4
The First Communion catechist introduces the topic of parties, and asks the children about their favourite party. She then goes on to tell them that the Mass is the best party ever, and that Jesus invites them to be there every week.

Example 5
After a powerful talk on human dignity, and how the prevailing secular culture threatens this dignity, the Confirmation candidates are led into a time of Adoration, with the opportunity to go to Confession.

Example 6
Before introducing the apologetics speaker who will explain Catholic teaching on some key moral issues, the Confirmation catechist asks the candidates to share their own views on each of the issues in small groups first.

Example 7
The RCIA catechist gives a thorough explanation of natural law. The catechumens evidently have many questions they are eager to ask, but they have run out of time and another group needs the room. The questions will have to wait till next week.

Example 8
One parish ensures that its RCIA process involves not just teaching. The catechumens are also introduced to liturgy in various forms, they have many opportunities to integrate into the parish community, and there is much time for prayer.

RECAP

- How would you explain to someone why it is important to be discerning about the methodology used for catechesis?
- What is meant by a "deductive" method and an "inductive" method?

JOURNALLING

- *Think about the methodology you typically use in your catechesis. Why did you choose this methodology?*
- *When you consider this methodology in the light of God's pedagogy, how does it stand up? Does it serve revelation and conversion? Can you give examples?*
- *If there is one change you would make to your current methodology, what would it be, and why?*

Serving or hindering God's revelation?

Below are comments on each of the examples we have considered in this chapter.

Example 1

• The Children's Liturgy seems to be very liturgical, linking it strongly to the Mass, and thereby emphasising to the children that they are still part of the Mass. This is shown in the procession out of the church, the liturgical setting with candle, Bible and icon, the gestures and words, and the way that the order of the liturgy follows the order of the Liturgy of the Word.

• The catechist's message following the Gospel proclaims the Word of God in a way that children will understand. This message, in being faithful both to God and to the human person, serves the unveiling of revelation.

• The time of quiet prayer at the end is at the service of conversion. We often shy away from quiet prayer with children, but experience shows it is possible if the environment is conducive to it, and if they are prepared well.

Example 2

• In this example, there is no content to the catechetical session, but already we see that first impressions and environmental factors either serve or hinder the pedagogy of God. The lack of welcome to the young people and the chaotic environment implicitly communicate that they are not worth more effort than this. Contrast instead an inviting welcome, a well-organised opening and hospitality shown towards each individual. Such a first impression – especially when consolidated week after week – communicates that God loves and is interested in them.

• Thanks to the game that flopped and the priest's sleep-inducing talk, it would seem, unfortunately, that the catechists have lost these teenagers from the start. They have been confirmed in their expectations that this experience will be boring. Already they have decided to make it more enjoyable by disrupting the sessions, and uniting together, they are sadly in danger of inoculating themselves against the impact of the Good News. From now on, these boys will be much harder to reach.

Example 3

• When we consider that God teaches "progressively", to cover these three major topics in the space of an hour and a half, when the candidates have likely not met before, is ambitious! Such an approach could prove to be overwhelming to candidates in the first week. What is more, unless they have attended an evangelisation course previously how can the catechists be sure they are ready for catechesis?

Example 4

• This is an example of the inductive method – the catechist begins with the children's experience in order to draw a connection with what is being taught. It is also an example of how the inductive method might not work very successfully. Seven-year-olds are unlikely to think that the Mass is as fun or exciting as parties they have been to. To emphasise the incomparability of the Mass, a deductive method might be more effective. This would show it is totally unique compared to other human activities

Example 5

• This is a great example of how to make catechesis sacramental and liturgical. The sacraments are where we meet Christ pre-eminently, and after a talk on a potentially moving and sensitive topic, the best thing we can do is take young people directly to him.

Example 6

• Here is another example of the inductive method being used badly. Our moral teachings are counter-cultural, and teenagers are likely to have imbibed the views of the culture rather than the Church. By allowing them to consolidate themselves in these views through sharing them in their small groups, the catechist is setting up the poor apologetics speaker to fail. The talk would have to be particularly powerful and convincing to win them over.

Example 7

• This is an example of the deductive method: the catechist explains the teaching directly. What is important about this method is that it be fully applied to everyday life. Without this, there is a danger that the teaching remains abstract and intellectually assented to, without having any real impact on the lives of the candidates. Without the chance to ask and answer questions, they will not be able to see what relevance this teaching holds for their lived experience.

Example 8

• Here is an example of a parish whose RCIA process attempts to touch all four dimensions of the Christian life (teaching, liturgy, life in Christ, prayer). By avoiding a programme made up only of classes, they are ensuring that the catechumens have a more integral experience, thereby increasing the likelihood of a deep conversion.

Chapter summary

- Catechesis not only serves the pedagogy of God but is inspired by it.

- The Church does not recommend any one methodology (*GDC* 148), but teaches that method should serve revelation and conversion, and guarantee fidelity to content (*GDC* 149).

- A method that is inspired by God's pedagogy is an integral formation; it reveals truth progressively; it makes use of both deductive and inductive approaches; it respects the dignity and freedom of the person.

HOLY SPIRIT, increase my insight and wisdom in creating sessions that will lead people to be open to you. Give me creativity, discernment and docility to work under your inspiration. AMEN.

CHAPTER 2:

Planning Sessions that Follow God's Pedagogy

I n Part 2, we offered step-by-step guidelines for preparing catechesis. In this chapter, we offer a methodology guide – a sample method for structuring catechesis. In the previous chapter, we considered some of the principles offered by the divine pedagogy which help guide session-planning. The Church affirms that no single method is preferred, but that all methods should be discerned in the light of God's pedagogy (*GDC* 148). Yet, it is helpful to have a framework to help plan a session. Understanding the principles behind the framework – and how it is inspired by the divine pedagogy – gives us flexibility to use and adapt it for different circumstances and audiences.

The framework is one developed by Mgr Francis Kelly in his book, *The Mystery We Proclaim.*[28] Mgr Kelly wanted to emphasise how a methodology inspired by the divine pedagogy is original and unique. To show how unique this method is to the Church's mission of handing on the faith, he named it "the ecclesial method".

Before diving into the ecclesial method, it is worth switching on the hazard lights for a moment. It is so easy for us to forget this vital point because we have become used to catechising

IN THIS CHAPTER...

• Explore one method for catechesis that follows the divine pedagogy – the ecclesial method.

• Understand how this method serves revelation and conversion.

people who don't have a relationship with God. "Frequently, many who present themselves for catechesis truly require genuine conversion" (*GDC* 62). *Catechesis is ineffective unless someone first has a relationship with God.* (Have a look again at Part 1, Chapter 3.) *If someone does not have a relationship with God* – or is not at least at the 'spiritual seeking' threshold of conversion – *evangelisation is required prior to catechesis.* The ecclesial method is *catechetical*, and works best with those who have a relationship with God. A different method is needed for those who do not:

• The ecclesial method begins and ends with prayer. This *does not make sense* unless a person desires to pray.

• People at the thresholds of trust through to openness are still in passive stages of indifference through to enquiry. At these stages, relationship-building and hospitality are far more fruitful than teaching.

• Far more effective for those at the early thresholds is the methodology used in various pre-evangelisation programmes (see 'Suggested Resources' on pg. 141): a meal, a talk or film, a discussion. Many of the details of this methodology (e.g. not correcting or teaching during the small groups) might feel counter-intuitive but in fact are very successful with such an audience.

• The ecclesial method, by contrast, presumes that a person has encountered Christ and desires to know him more. Without this initial faith, it is unlikely to make an impact and may even push someone who is at the early stages of conversion away.

The ecclesial method
Step One: Preparation
As we saw in the examples of the last chapter, first impressions count. What do people find when they arrive? Is the environment calm and ordered, creating the conditions for an encounter with God, or are catechists rushing around finishing off last-minute preparations? Mgr Kelly suggests that the aim should be "calculated disengagement". We want participants to be able to "disengage" from what they have come from (busyness, noise, demands) and prepare to hear God's word. The environment is deliberately different. It implicitly states: catechesis is something different. *It is not just more learning like the rest of your day; here you are coming into God's presence.*

HOW TO DO IT:
• For young people, have an activity for them to join in with as soon as they enter the room, for example a game, or a prompt for them to write in their spiritual journal (e.g. "How have I experienced God in my life this week?"). The start time of the session should be definite and lead straight into a time of prayer.

• For adults, for example RCIA, have refreshments as people arrive, and begin promptly with a time of prayer. This could include a Liturgy of the Word.

- For children, it helps to have a separate area that is reserved for prayer and catechesis. Instinctively they know as they enter this area that they will spend time with God.

CATECHIST TESTIMONY

"Having a display with sacred art (known as 'sacred space') indicates that something different, something special is happening at a particular meeting, that God's message is about to be echoed. My go-to resource for sacred space is Rublev's The hospitality of Abraham *(Gn 18). While this fifteenth-century icon ignites our senses with its rich colours, its main purpose is to connect us with God, with the divine. Just as God slowly and progressively revealed himself to us through the Old Testament, this beautiful icon can be referred to again and again to slowly unfold the central tenets of our faith. The opening in the centre front invites us to join in the loving relationship, that inner life of our Almighty God. Indeed, we are personally invited into relationship with the Blessed Trinity! The three angelic figures with identical faces and blue garments, manifesting One God: the Father, Christ His Son and the Holy Spirit, are gathered around a table. While the Holy Spirit on the right inclines us into the central figure, Christ (with his earthy brown and blue garments to link heaven and earth) is gazing back at his heavenly Father. The eyes of the three clearly denote a circular motion – the movement of love. Just as the three persons are in communion, our relationship is nourished at the table of the Lord."*

Margaret Wickware, St Luke's Parish, Pinner

Step 2: Proclamation

In the Guide to Preparing Catechesis in Part 2, the idea of the Proclamation was introduced. The Proclamation is the most important step of the whole catechesis. It is an announcement, loud and bold, joyful and convicted: "If you remember anything at all – this is the message I want you to hear." In Part 1, Chapter 1, we considered how the kerygma is the "first proclamation", the quick, breathless message that you want someone to hear first, before you go into the details. Fr Raniero Cantalamessa summed it up well when he wrote:

> The runner arriving breathlessly in the town square from the battlefield doesn't begin by giving an orderly account of the development of event and neither does he waste time on details. He goes straight to the point and in a few words gives the most vital piece of news which everyone is waiting to hear. Explanations can come later. If a battle has been won, he shouts: 'Victory!' and if peace has been made, he shouts: 'Peace!'
>
> (*Life in the Lordship of Jesus Christ* (London: Darton,Longman & Todd Ltd, 1992) p.1)

Look back at Part 2 at the suggested Proclamations for the Blessed Trinity, the dignity of the human person, Jesus Christ, the Paschal Mystery, and the Church. Each one expresses the heart of the teaching in a way that is memorable, that you can come back to frequently through the catechesis.

HOW TO DO IT:

• Know the message you are going to proclaim. Keep it short, concise and easy to remember.

• Internalise it, so you can proclaim it with confidence and joy.

• Ensure it is age appropriate, that the words will be understood or easily explained to your audience.

• Keep returning to this message through the catechesis.

• If it is memorisable, encourage your group to repeat phrases back to you. Memory is a great, but often under-utilised, gift in catechesis.

• Try writing some sample Proclamations for the audience you normally work with. Write one for each of the following teachings: the Eucharist, salvation history, Our Lady.

Step 3: Explanation

This is where you unpack the Proclamation in such a way that your audience begins to understand this truth for themselves. It is likely to be the longest step of the catechesis and it is where you will use your ingenuity and skill, with the Holy Spirit, to unveil the meaning of this message, so that your audience understands and internalises it too. Many examples and ideas are listed in Part 2 under each of the teachings explored there.

HOW TO DO IT:

• Since the Explanation is the longest step, you will want to break it down into chunks. Be aware of the longest length of time your audience can listen before drifting off. For teenagers, this is likely to be 10-15 minutes, while for adults you can maybe stretch to 20 minutes. The more actively learners participate, the more they will be engaged.

• Make use of a wide range of communication tools: storytelling, question and answer, repetition of key words and phrases, role-play, sacred art, testimonies, analogies with everyday experience, dialogue between catechists and participants, short film clips, memorable props.

• Be aware of different learning preferences: people learn differently, for example through hearing, or seeing, or doing.

• Keep returning to the Proclamation.

Step 4: Application

Remember the response of those who heard Peter's speech in Acts 2? They asked him, "What are we do to?" (*Ac* 2:37) When we are presented with the truth, we not only want to assent to it intellectually, we feel compelled to change the way we live. Mgr Kelly suggests that in this step of the catechesis, our aim is "calculated re-engagement". We want our audience to re-engage with their experience. *If this is true, what does this mean for my life?*

Often, this response is very personal. Imagine a person who is prone to anxiety hearing a teaching on the over-abundant love and attentiveness of God the Father. The Holy Spirit moves in their heart and they realise, "Wow! Why do I worry so much if God is my Father?" Or imagine someone who has been struggling with sin hearing a talk on the power of grace. They are led to a powerful moment when they desire to ask the Lord for more grace to help them fight this battle. Or a person who feels alone and tries to fill their loneliness with unhealthy relationships. They hear teaching on how, through Baptism, the three Persons of the Trinity dwell within them. They realise that, truly, they are never alone.

HOW TO DO IT:

- Moments of silence for reflection
- Carefully led small group discussion
- Personal journalling
- An opportunity to speak with someone one-to-one (normally outside catechesis)
- Encouragement to make specific resolutions.

Step 5: Celebration

End on a high. The sessions began with prayer and expectation that God would act. Through the catechesis, he has been speaking and revealing himself. It is therefore only right to thank and praise God – to cultivate an attitude of gratitude and worship essential for the life of a Christian. Maybe there has been confusion or even scepticism in people's hearts during the session. In ending on a note of praise, we offer everything – even our doubt – to God. This is the moment when we can make it abundantly clear who is the One who guides and forms us.

HOW TO DO IT:

- If possible, move into a different place – ideally, the church. Bringing people into the presence of Jesus in the Blessed Sacrament puts them into contact with the One with whom we want them to have intimacy and communion.

- Use music. Music has a powerful role in the Christian life in moving us to adore, meditate and contemplate.

- Model prayer. Lead the group by demonstrating how we can speak intimately with the Lord: "Lord, thank you for all we heard today. Thank you for the gift of the Eucharist – that you are present to us in your Body, Blood, Soul and Divinity."

• Introduce traditions of the Church's prayer: the Rosary, the Liturgy of the Hours, the Stations of the Cross.

• Use silence. We can be nervous about silence – especially with young children. But silence is the language of God and without it many powerful encounters may be missed. Escape the tyranny of noise and allow people to experience silence.

Chapter summary

- One method that follows the pedagogy of God is the ecclesial method. This is a catechetical method and presupposes that a person already has a relationship with God, and is at least at the threshold of spiritual seeking.

- The five steps of the ecclesial method transmit the faith in a way that respects participants' freedom while inviting them to conversion, and ensures that revelation is passed on "in its entirety" (CT 58).

JESUS, how deeply you long to enter our hearts!
Show us how great your desire is to encounter each
person. Increase our expectation of how you long
to use catechesis as a place for transformation. AMEN.

Methodology Guide

Session Title: _____   Session Length: _____

Last Week's Session:_____   Catechists: _____

Next Week's Session: _____

Catechist Preparation

Audience: Where are they in terms of discipleship?

TRUST	CURIOSITY	OPENNESS	SEEKING	BEGINNING DISCIPLE	GROWING DISCIPLE	COMMISSIONED DISCIPLE	DISCIPLE MAKER	SPIRITUAL MULTIPLIER

Given where the audience is in terms of discipleship, here's what I should consider when planning the session (look back at Part 1, Chapter 2):

_____

_____

_____

Scripture for this topic:	CCC for this topic:

Lectio Divina:

Scripture: _____

Your reflection:

Proclamation:

How does the session topic relate to the kerygma?

_____

_____

3-5 Teaching Points:

1.

2.

3.

4.

5.

Environment (room layout, music, display):

Catechist Roles

Hospitality/Refreshments:

Tech:

Welcoming:

Small Group Leaders:

Session Plan

	TIME	WHO?
1. PREPARATION		
2. PROCLAMATION		
3. EXPLANATION		
4. APPLICATION		
5. CELEBRATION		

CHAPTER 3:

Practical Leadership

It should be dazzlingly clear that the Holy Spirit working through you – your personality, natural talents and spiritual charisms – is the key to effective catechesis. Without a doubt, God has bestowed you with:

• A unique and irreplaceable personality

• Tremendous natural strengths (see www.gallupstrengths center.com for a helpful strengths finder assessment).

• Awe-inspiring spiritual charisms of the Holy Spirit (see www.siena.org to find out more about the Called and Gifted programme and discerning your charisms).

When we are growing in relationship with God, listening to him daily, and trying to live according to his will, this can become a potent mix. Don't underestimate what God wants to do through you.

Growing as a catechist

As we increase in catechetical experience, here are some different ways we grow.

1) Feedback

The most valuable experience I have gained as a catechist is teaching in front of others – sometimes repeatedly – and receiving their feedback. It is not normal in the Church to give feedback on teaching or preaching – but in the teaching profession and other Christian communities it is. If you want to grow as a catechist, *beg* others for feedback! Perhaps you have a strange habit of standing in a certain way while public speaking. Perhaps the way you told a story didn't get the message across as clearly as it could have done. Only feedback in a spirit of love and trust will help you improve.

2) Observing others

As catechists, we find ourselves watching others give talks in a whole new light. Who are the speakers you admire and who inspire you? Watch them teach and think about how they structure their talk, how they engage their audience, how they use humour, silence or interaction, how they lead people to encounter Christ.

3) Building relationships

In my early days as a catechist, I was happy to teach – and sometimes hide behind my teaching. Many people I taught in RCIA were older than I was, and I didn't know how to build relationships with them. As I have grown older and more confident, I see relationships with the people I am teaching as the foundation of catechesis. People move through the early thresholds thanks to friendship, community and hospitality – more than teaching. If people have a trusting relationship with you, if you have shared your life with them and let them in, how much more convincing will they find your catechesis?

Several programmes use the methodology of a meal, talk, and a film or small discussion group. It can be uncomfortable at the outset because it invites people to share their thoughts on a topic without jumping in to correct or teach them the truth. It feels counter-intuitive, but my experience has been that – if we follow this approach, showing people that we care what they think and accept them as they are – they are far more open later when we offer catechesis and lead them into the mysteries of what God has revealed. When it comes to teaching hard truths, are people more likely to accept these from a distant teacher who does not give much of their own life away, or from a friend?

4) Disciple-making

Relationship-building should come with an occupational warning. You will soon find that your phone is stuffed with numbers of people who are in your evangelising radar. St Paul "discipled" Timothy and we see his counsel to him in the First and Second Letters to Timothy. Paul tells Timothy, "What you have heard from me before many witnesses entrust to faithful men who will be able to teach others also" (*2 Tm* 2:2). We all need a St Paul (someone to disciple or mentor us) and we should also have many Timothies – people whom we are discipling and mentoring. The Discipleship Roadmap outlines how a growing disciple is one who will make any sacrifice to grow. But a commissioned disciple is one who will make any sacrifice to help another person grow. Will we change our plans to schedule coffee with someone God has entrusted to us? Will we drive to another town to take someone to an event we know will help them? Will we send a copy of a book to someone who could use it? Will we go to additional Sunday Masses just to make contact with someone we think might be slipping away? The extent to which we are willing to make sacrifices is a good measure of the extent to which we have embraced our missionary calling.

5) Skilful discussion leading

We all know the pitfalls of a small-group discussion: the person who dominates; the people who remain quiet; the reticence about sharing anything too deep. The awkward Britishness of it! But when a discussion group takes off, it can be unparalleled in moving people forward through the thresholds. I have known small groups where, despite awkward beginnings, people gradually opened up and, before we knew it, shared a social media group, were praying for each other, and still meet regularly to this day. There is nothing better than Christian community to keep us on the road of discipleship.

If you are leading a small group, keep it light-hearted from the beginning. Connect with people on topics other than faith. If you can share a meal together, all the better. Avoid intensity, intra-ecclesial politics and hot-button topics. Avoid presuming anything of people's knowledge of the Church or faith, or of their relationship with God. The best small groups I have experienced are the ones where there is most laughter.

Keeping conversation normal and light will increase the trust of those in the early thresholds. If they are able to think "Wow, this is a normal group of people I would like

to spend time with" – rather than a bunch of slightly eccentric, ecclesiastical bores! – you are winning. Increasing trust creates an environment where honesty will prevail. People will be more willing to share truthfully what they don't know or struggle to believe. Demonstrate vulnerability by sharing your own experience – without revealing anything too personal or heavy. Above all, pray for the Holy Spirit to fill your conversation. Model this prayer by praying aloud at the beginning or end of the group.

6) Spiritual discernment

The origins of the word "discernment" mean "to cut away". Discernment is the process of hearing the voice of God through the noise of many other motivations that pull us in different directions. Developing our ability to discern is indispensable for growth in interior life, and the Church has a rich tradition of spiritual advice. One such source is the Rules of St Ignatius: an excellent podcast series, *Discernment of Spirits* by Fr Timothy Gallagher, is available at www.discerninghearts.com. As we become more perceptive to the movements of the Holy Spirit in our own lives we find ourselves more able to listen to others too. As catechists, we are not spiritual directors or counsellors. Our parish priest should make decisions regarding readiness for sacraments or when someone should move into the next stage of RCIA. But our own discernment may become a resource the priest can depend on: threshold conversations require a careful listening ear; determining what individuals need in order to move forward; deciding who would be a good sponsor or small-group leader for particular people.

Programme organisation

When we have a clearer vision of the purpose of catechesis to make disciples, we start becoming aware that certain models we have traditionally used in the parish are unhelpful in achieving our goals. From all you have read so far, it might be becoming clearer that the following practices are helpful at making disciples:

- One-to-one friendships where we help each other grow as disciples.

- Vibrant community where a relationship with God is the norm and openly talked about.

- Various overlapping opportunities to hear the kerygma in multiple ways and contexts.

This requires a shift in parish culture, which is beyond the remit of this book. But the fruitfulness of catechesis in your parish will undoubtedly be significantly influenced by your parish's discipleship culture (or lack of one). The following are practices that are likely to hinder your disciple-making efforts:

- Programmes of fixed duration with no discernment of individual needs or growth.

- Catechesis that does not expect or bring about personal transformation.

- Catechesis that remains at the level of opinion sharing, without allowing the transformative power of revelation to be heard and accepted.

• An outlook that sees relationship with God as private and not to be shared in community.

The reality is that, while a shift in parish culture will come about only through a shift to new, creative models of handing on the faith, many of us still have to work within the model of traditional sacramental programmes. Whatever model your parish is using, the timeline below is designed to help your planning.

Timeline

TIME BEFORE PROGRAMME STARTS	GOALS
6 MONTHS	1) Review last year's programme • Did it move people forward in terms of thresholds of conversion? Why/why not? • What were the strong elements to the programme? Team; content; method; time allocated; venue. How can these be built on? • What were its weaknesses? How can they be resolved? 2) Outline a plan for next year's programme.
4 MONTHS	1) Identify prayer support for the programme • How can you ensure that the programme is underpinned by prayer? Is there a prayer group in your parish? Those with a charism for intercessory prayer? Or could the housebound or elderly be asked to pray? Could you assign each participant a prayer partner who will dedicate to pray for them? 2) Finalise catechetical team • Identify main catechists (those with strong theological knowledge and communication skills). • Identify helpers – those who can help with hospitality, tech, leading prayer, room layout, small-group leaders (some of these helpers may train as future catechists). • If your programme is with children, do you have a sufficient ratio of adults to children? • Check all DBS checks are up-to-date and get the ball rolling with new checks.

4 MONTHS	**3)** Schedule dates for the year
	• Check school holidays in your area.
	• If you are organising a retreat, some venues need to be booked a year in advance.
	• Publicise dates well in advance to help families with planning, including dates for parents.
	4) Advertise and open enrolment for programme
	• Decide what the requirements will be for enrolment and clearly advertise these: Will you accept only children or teens who go to Mass regularly? Is there an expectation that they will attend every date in the programme?
	• Consider meeting each family individually as part of the enrolment process. Consider what kind of questions you could pose to initiate a threshold conversation (see *Forming Intentional Disciples*, pp. 191-199).
	• Decide when the deadline will be.
1 MONTH	**1)** Gather team together for prayer and planning
	• Ensure you have enough time for prayer and fellowship with your team. Building a team culture will flow into the programme itself.
	• Delegate tasks and ensure everyone knows what is expected of them.
	• Identify dates through the year when you will review how the programme is going.

Tips for a fruitful session

Hospitality

Hospitality is a disarmingly simple yet effective tool in the evangelisation toolbox. When winning people in the early thresholds, who can resist a warm and genuine welcome, an attentiveness which reveals all at once our personal interest, the care of the Church and – most importantly – the love of God? Walk step-by-step through a person's arrival at your catechetical programme, considering what their experience will be. A team based outside at the entrance to welcome expresses our joy that they have come. Ensuring that no one is ever standing or sitting alone demonstrates our love. Starting on time, being fully prepared, thinking through details in advance – all demonstrate that we value participants and the time they have given.

Technology

In many Catholic parishes, this can be an area of weakness. Maybe your church hall doesn't have Wi-Fi, or showing any film involves a cumbersome process of locating multiple items of equipment, cables trailing in every direction. If we are serious about evangelising those saturated in our culture (not just the young!), we need to get savvier at matching their cultural expectations. Investing in quality audio-visual (and Wi-Fi) for your church is an investment in evangelisation. The normal medium for communication is increasingly film and having a strong AV system means we can use this medium effortlessly without tech problems that impair people's experience.

Prayer

Allocate one team member to prepare the time of prayer for each session. Always opt for authentic expressions of Catholic prayer that develop a person's relationship with God. Try to pray in the presence of the Blessed Sacrament as far as possible. Demonstrate reverence and silence, and know that your demeanour in church speaks louder than anything you might teach about the Eucharist.

Room layout

Consider carefully how to lay out the room. If you have a large Confirmation group, what room layout will serve maximum attention? Consider allocating groups and seats to ensure a sense of order. Think about having a focal point to set the scene for the session. Put yourself in a participant's shoes: what will they be looking at, what will they be hearing?

Chapter summary

- God has bestowed us with natural strengths as well as – thanks to our Baptism and Confirmation – supernatural charisms.

- Whatever our combination of strengths and charisms, we can grow and improve as catechists through a range of human and spiritual means.

- Good planning is essential for catechesis to be as effective and fruitful as possible.

HOLY SPIRIT, increase in me apostolic zeal, gifts of discernment and a persevering spirit. Keep me constant in prayer. Equip me to bring many people to know Jesus. AMEN.

CHAPTER 4:
Resource Evaluation Tool

Just because a catechetical resource is published does not mean it presents the faith integrally, in its entirety or following the pedagogy of God. We have a responsibility to evaluate a resource before we start using it. While the previous chapters in Part 3 should help you evaluate the methodology of a resource, the following tool should help you evaluate the content.

NAME OF RESOURCE	CATECHETICAL AREA	RECOMMENDATIONS

GOD THE TRINITY

• Does this resource refer throughout to God, Father, Son and Holy Spirit?

Very Good ☐   *Good* ☐   *Satisfactory* ☐   *Needs to be supplemented* ☐

• Does it show the persons of the Trinity to be one undivided God?

Very Good ☐   *Good* ☐   *Satisfactory* ☐   *Needs to be supplemented* ☐

• Are the persons of the Trinity presented equal in divinity?

Very Good ☐   *Good* ☐   *Satisfactory* ☐   *Needs to be supplemented* ☐

CENTRALITY OF JESUS CHRIST IN SALVATION HISTORY

• Does the resource show the unfolding of God's plan from Creation and the Old Testament to its fulfilment in Christ in the New Testament?

Very Good ☐   *Good* ☐   *Satisfactory* ☐   *Needs to be supplemented* ☐

• Is Jesus Christ clearly presented to be true God and true Man?

Very Good ☐   *Good* ☐   *Satisfactory* ☐   *Needs to be supplemented* ☐

• Are Jesus and the Gospel Message central throughout the resource?

Very Good ☐   *Good* ☐   *Satisfactory* ☐   *Needs to be supplemented* ☐

• Are the saving actions of Jesus clearly presented and explained? (His Life, Passion, Death, Resurrection and Ascension)

Very Good ☐   *Good* ☐   *Satisfactory* ☐   *Needs to be supplemented* ☐

THE CHURCH

- Is the Church seen to be connected to Jesus Christ as his body, the place of communion with God through the Holy Spirit?

  Very Good ☐   *Good* ☐   *Satisfactory* ☐   *Needs to be supplemented* ☐

- Is the priest seen as acting in the person of Christ in conferring the sacraments?

  Very Good ☐   *Good* ☐   *Satisfactory* ☐   *Needs to be supplemented* ☐

- Is the Church presented as God's loving plan for us, necessary for our salvation?

  Very Good ☐   *Good* ☐   *Satisfactory* ☐   *Needs to be supplemented* ☐

DIGNITY OF THE HUMAN PERSON

- Is it clear that we are created by God and for God out of love, in his image and likeness?

  Very Good ☐   *Good* ☐   *Satisfactory* ☐   *Needs to be supplemented* ☐

- Is it clear that in baptism we become children of the Father, members of Christ and temples of the Holy Spirit ?

  Very Good ☐   *Good* ☐   *Satisfactory* ☐   *Needs to be supplemented* ☐

- Is it clear that we are restored to our original dignity through Christ after being disfigured by sin?

  Very Good ☐   *Good* ☐   *Satisfactory* ☐   *Needs to be supplemented* ☐

GRACE – BEING ALIVE IN JESUS CHRIST

- Does the resource aim to foster an interior personal relationship with Jesus Christ?

  Very Good ☐   *Good* ☐   *Satisfactory* ☐   *Needs to be supplemented* ☐

- Does the resource emphasises the transformative action of God in our life?

  Very Good ☐   *Good* ☐   *Satisfactory* ☐   *Needs to be supplemented* ☐

- Does the resource mention the action and power of the Holy Spirit?

  Very Good ☐   *Good* ☐   *Satisfactory* ☐   *Needs to be supplemented* ☐

- Are the gifts of faith, hope and charity emphasised? (examples of the Saints)

  Very Good ☐   *Good* ☐   *Satisfactory* ☐   *Needs to be supplemented* ☐

SACRAMENTS – MEANS BY WHICH WE SHARE IN THE LIFE OF CHRIST

• Are the sacraments presented both as signs and cause of grace? As divine means of transformation in Christ?

Very Good ☐   *Good* ☐   *Satisfactory* ☐   *Needs to be supplemented* ☐

• Are the sacraments linked with the Death and Resurrection of Jesus?

Very Good ☐   *Good* ☐   *Satisfactory* ☐   *Needs to be supplemented* ☐

• Is the Mass explained to be the sacrifice of Christ on the Cross made present for us?

Very Good ☐   *Good* ☐   *Satisfactory* ☐   *Needs to be supplemented* ☐

• Is the real presence of Christ sufficiently emphasised in the Eucharist?

Very Good ☐   *Good* ☐   *Satisfactory* ☐   *Needs to be supplemented* ☐

ORIGINAL SIN

• Is there reference to original sin and sufficient explanation of its consequences i.e. We need to be brought back into friendship and union with God?

Very Good ☐   *Good* ☐   *Satisfactory* ☐   *Needs to be supplemented* ☐

• Is this linked to God's saving action reaching us in Baptism and the other sacraments?

Very Good ☐   *Good* ☐   *Satisfactory* ☐   *Needs to be supplemented* ☐

CHRISTIAN MORAL LIFE

• Is Jesus Christ seen as the model for our daily lives?

Very Good ☐   *Good* ☐   *Satisfactory* ☐   *Needs to be supplemented* ☐

• Are the words of life found in the double commandment of love, the Ten Commandments and the Beatitudes presented as the Christian rule of life?

Very Good ☐   *Good* ☐   *Satisfactory* ☐   *Needs to be supplemented* ☐

END TIMES

• Is sufficient emphasis placed on looking forward to eternal life in communion with God and the Saints in heaven?

Very Good ☐   *Good* ☐   *Satisfactory* ☐   *Needs to be supplemented* ☐

CHAPTER 5:

Suggested Resources

Evangelisation of adults (initial proclamation)
- Sycamore – thinking about life and faith (www.sycamore.fm)
- Discovering Christ (www.christlife.org)
- The Gift – a Life in the Spirit course (www.ccr.org.uk)
- Alpha in a Catholic Context (www.alpha.org/catholics)*

Discipleship and catechesis for adults
- CCO Faith Study Series (www.cco.ca)
- Anchor (www.anchoryourfaith.com)
- Symbolon (www.symboloncatholic.org)
- House on Rock (www.houseonrock.co.uk)
- The Bible Timeline (www.biblestudyforcatholics.com)
- Evangelium (www.evangelium.co.uk)
- Word on Fire – Catholicism series (www.wordonfire.org)
- The Sacraments (www.faithcafe.org)

RCIA
- Association for Catechumenal Ministry (www.acmrcia.org)
- Many of the above resources can be used for RCIA.

Youth resources
- YDisciple (www.formed.org)
- T3 Bible Timeline (www.ascensionpress.com)
- YOU: Life, Love and the Theology of the Body (www.ascensionpress.com)
- Life Teen (www.lifeteen.com)
- Altaration (www.ascensionpress.com)
- Youth Alpha (www.alpha.org/alpha-youth-series)*

Confirmation
- YouCat Confirmation Book (www.youcat.org)
- Transformed in Christ (www.transformedinchrist.com)
- Chosen (www.ascensionpress.com)
- Decision Point (www.dynamiccatholic.com)

*Alpha is a Protestant evangelical course in the basics of Christianity that originated at Holy Trinity Brompton, an Anglican church. It was popularised in the 1990s by Nicky Gumbel as a tool of evangelisation.

Children's resources

- Come Follow Me (www.comefollowme.info)
- Catechesis of the Good Shepherd (www.cgsuk.org)
- Godly Play (www.godlyplay.uk)
- Brother Francis (www.brotherfrancisonline.com)
- Virtues in Practice (www.nashvilledominican.org)
- Faith and Life (www.ignatius.com)

First Reconciliation and Communion

- I want to make my home in you (*Come Follow Me* resource from Redemptorist Publications)
- Called to His Supper (Our Sunday Visitor)
- Jesus Comes to Me (Redemptorist Publications)

Children's liturgy

- Liturgy of the Word with Children (www.liturgyoffice.org.uk/Resources/LOWC/index.shtml)
- The Sunday Book of Readings (McCrimmons)
- The Liturgy of the Word with Children (Kevin Mayhew)
- The Wednesday Word (www.wednesdayword.org)

Baptism

- Belonging: Baptism in the Family of God (www.ascensionpress.com)
- Reborn (www.formed.org)

Marriage

- Beloved – Mystery and Meaning of Marriage (www.formed.org)
- Engaged (www.smartloving.org)
- The Sacraments – Marriage (www.faithcafe.org)
- The Marriage Course (www.themarriagecourses.org)

Online platforms sharing wealth of resources (including many listed above):

- www.formed.org
- www.ascensionpress.com

ENDNOTES

[1] See Bullivant, S. (2016) "Contemporary Catholicism in England and Wales: A statistical report based on British Social Attitudes survey data". (Benedict XVI Centre for Religion and Society, St Mary's University, Twickenham).

[2] Ibid.

[3] Bruce, S. (2014) "Late Secularisation and Religion as Alien". (Open Theology 2014; Volume 1: 13-23).

[4] See studies by Katz and Lazarsfeld (1964).

[5] Read their story in Mallon, J. (2014) *Divine Renovation*. (New London: Twenty-Third Publications).

[6] Benedict XVI, Homily during the Prayer Vigil with Young People at Cuatro Vientos Air Base, Madrid, 26th World Youth Day, 20 August 2011.

[7] Adapted from Schaupp, Dougg (1998) *Five Thresholds of Post-Modern Conversion*.

[8] www.latintimes.com/eduardo-verastegui-questions-if-marriage-gods-plan-him-after-14-years-celibacy- 383172

[9] Weddell, Sherry (2012) *Forming Intentional Disciples*, p. 157.

[10] *Forming Intentional Disciples*, p. 178.

[11] Based on FOCUS resource, Discipleship Roadmap: www.focusoncampus.org/content/discipleship-road-map

[12] For more, see Mgr Eugene Kevane (1982) *Teaching the Faith Today*.

[13] *The Mystery We Proclaim*, p. 44. (Eugene, Oregon: Wipf and Stock, 1999).

[14] See Willey, Petroc (2011) "The Pedagogue and the Teacher" in *The Pedagogy of God* (Steubenville, Ohio: Emmaus Road Publishing), p. 42.

[15] Based on FOCUS resource, Discipleship Roadmap: www.focusoncampus.org/content/discipleship-road-map

[16] From *Why Catholics Leave, What They Miss, and How They Might Return* (2018, forthcoming: Paulist Press).

[17] Three such resources are the Association for Catechumenal Ministry's RCIA process, the *Transformed in Christ* Confirmation programme, and the *Faith and Life* textbook series for primary-school-age catechesis.

[18] For more information on identifying teaching points from the Catechism, see Willey, Petroc "The Catechism & the New Evangelisation: Lesson Planning with the Catechism", Parts 1 and 2, *The Catechetical Review*, Issues 2.1 and 2.2.

[19] In every edition of the quarterly publication *The Catechetical Review* is a series called "Art Notes". It introduces a piece of sacred art with a commentary that can be used in catechesis.

[20] For more on catechising with the Sign of the Cross, see Willey, Petroc "Catechesis on the Sign of the Cross" in *The Sower*, Issue 30.2.

[21] See *Transformed in Christ* Confirmation programme, Session 19.

[22] www.washingtonpost.com/news/the-switch/wp/2015/11/03/teens-spend-nearly-nine-hours-every-day-consuming-media/?utm_term=.5527008a2271

[23] See www.grassrootsfilms.com/thehumanexperience/

[24] www.comefollowme.info

[25] To read more about Jesus's Death fulfilling the Passover, read Pope Benedict XVI's *Jesus of Nazareth: Holy Week*, Chapter 5.

[26] See www.cco.ca

[27] Cf. Payne and Whittaker, 2000.

[28] *The Mystery We Proclaim*, Chapter 3.

PICTURE CREDITS

Cover image: *The Baptism of Christ*, c.1623. Artist: Reni, Guido (1575-1642) Art History Museum, Vienna, Austria. © Fine Art Images | Heritage Images | Getty Images.

Page 5: Overkit; **8**: Photogolfer; **14**: Denis Kuvaev; **17**: Meunierd; **18**: Renata Sedmakova; **22**: Rawpixel.com; **36 & 86**: Everett - Art; **53**: Antracit; **54**: Renata Sedmakova; **57**: Wideonet; **62**: Koval Nadiya; **70**: Jorisvo; **79**: Adam Jan Figel; **93**: Pres Panayotov; **106**: Nomad Fra; **106**: Monkey Business Images; **112**: Biletskiy; **121**: Creative Lab; **132**: GaudiLab. All images from Shutterstock.com.

Page 11: © Mazur/catholicnews.org.uk

Page 39: Roland Pargeter; **41 & 64**: Robertharding; **49**: Pacific Press; **99**: Photononstop. All images from Alamy Stock Photos.